Tennis Everyone
Sixth Edition

M.B. Chafin
and
Roland Thornqvist

*University of Florida
Gainesville, Florida*

Tom Daglis

*Ferris State University
Grand Rapids, Michigan*

The Rules of Tennis appearing in the Appendix were provided by the United States Tennis Association and are reprinted with permission.

The photo of the Newport Casino and the historical photos appearing in Chapter 1 were made available through the assistance of the International Tennis Hall of Fame and Tennis Museum, Newport, Rhode Island.

Printed in the United States of America

ISBN 0-88725-328-8

 Hunter Textbooks Inc.

701 Shallowford Street
Winston-Salem, NC 27102
www.huntertextbooks.com

ACKNOWLEDGMENTS

The Authors would like to express deep appreciation to several individuals who assisted in the revision of this book. Sincere thanks are in order to Mike Chafin, Steve Beeland, Louise Fletcher, Naomi Davies, Roland Thornqvist, David Balogh, Jeremy Bayon, and Robert Taylor who spent many hours on the courts as subjects for photographs; to Bill Cross, John Gerber, Carlos Muniz and Paul McKinley for posing for the doubles photo; and to Sue Packing for participating in photographs. The authors are also grateful to Mike Floyd, owner of Court Side Sports for allowing the use of his well-equipped tennis shop. Appreciation is also extended to Curtis Weldon, who was the photographer for this revised edition. Also to the University of Florida Athletic Association - Sports Publicity Department for the use of the pictures of the Alfred E. Ring Tennis Complex.

Table of Contents

Tennis—Today and Yesterday

WHY TENNIS?

At this point you are probably asking yourself, "Why did I choose tennis?" Or perhaps you are already an occasional player and are asking the question, "Why do I continue to play this crazy, frustrating game?"

Whatever your reason, it is possible that in the next few weeks you will arrive at a decision that will affect your lifestyle and habits for the remainder of your life. However, if by chance you should decide that the game of tennis is not for you, at least the decision will be made on the basis of sound information and a fair trial.

As a non-contact sport, tennis offers a wide range of diverse benefits to all participants. First and foremost, the game is one of motor skill requiring a strong emphasis on hand-eye coordination with a corresponding emphasis on speed, strength, endurance and agility. This in no way minimizes the fact that the ability to strike a tennis ball correctly is fundamental to long-range success. Equally important is the mental aspect to the game, one that is not found in many other athletic endeavors. It is impossible to be a winning tennis player and not be reasonably intelligent. Additionally, you must possess the ability to calculate while engaged in a fiercely contested point. It has been said that tennis requires more mental involvement from its participants than any other sport.

While many tennis matches have been decided on the endurance level of the players, one of the best aspects of the game is that it can be adapted to the participant's age, sex and level of competition. Like checkers players, older participants frequently develop a seasoned degree of gamesmanship, which offers some compensation for legs that may have lost their youthful spring. The doubles game can also be enjoyed as long as a person can maintain some degree of mobility. Tennis, as with some other sports, also has its own handicapping system. Should you feel you are too accomplished to play with someone, try beginning each game with a one- or two-point deficit and see how quickly the competition is evened!

In terms of a fitness activity, tennis is decidedly better for you than most other sports. Discounting running and swimming, which burn more calories but are boring and repetitious, tennis probably offers more advantages than any other activity. Approximately 40 million people in the United States alone have decided that burning up to 500 calories an hour, increasing muscle strength without a great increase in muscle size, releasing tension in a wholesome manner, and socializing both for business and pleasure are definitely to their liking. Most also agree that tennis is fun; therefore, it is their answer to the current fitness drive. Tennis is played throughout the world, and the nature of the game is such that both sexes can compete with and against each other.

Another aspect of tennis that has remained through the years is the capacity for developing true sportsmanship despite the intense competitive nature of the game. The cheating tennis player is an oddity rather than the rule, and whenever players do not conform to the unwritten code, they are quickly abandoned by other players.

By this time, you may be convinced that tennis is the game for you and you are anxious to get on the courts. However, there are several points to consider.

First, tennis need not cost you a lot of money. If you choose to join a private club, play at night or indoors and purchase the most expensive equipment, the cost could amount to a considerable sum of money. However, if you play on public courts and select moderately priced equipment, the game will cost considerably less than golfing, skiing or boating.

Tennis dress of yesteryear

Second, tennis requires a commitment of time if you really want to improve your skill level. It is not one of the easiest games to master, however, almost everyone who perseveres can become reasonably adept at striking the ball. They may not look and play like professionals, but they will derive many of the same benefits that keep most tennis players returning to the courts year after year. Another caution: Once "hooked" you will probably play the game for the rest of your life!

ORIGIN OF THE GAME

The history of ancient civilizations indicates that a form of tennis was probably played by the early Greeks and Romans. Other evidence indicates that the Chinese were batting a ball back and forth more than 7,000 years ago, and that the Egyptians and Persians also played some kind of a ball and racket game as early as 500 B.C.

The most solid and recent evidence, however, indicates a tennis-like game being played in France about 1200 A.D. The French game called *jeu de paume*, or "game of the hand," consisted of hitting a stuffed object over a rope with the bare hand. Rackets did not make an appearance until about 1400 A.D. England and Holland had both accepted the sport by this time and Chaucer referred to the game by using the present name, which is probably a derivative of the French word *tenez*. The game prospered greatly in France and England. However, the French Revolution almost obliterated the sport, since at that time it was considered a game of the rich.

These earliest contests did not much resemble our present game. It was not until 1873 that Walter C. Wingfield, a British army major, introduced a new outdoor game which, while incorporating many other aspects, was more similar to our present grass court game. He chose to name his game *sphairistike*, a Greek word meaning "to play." Since the name was too difficult to pronounce, let alone spell, the English quickly began calling the game "tennis on the lawn" and eventually lawn tennis.

The game quickly spread throughout the British empire, and in 1874, Mary Outerbridge, who was vacationing in Bermuda, brought the game with her to New York. As a member of the Staten Island Cricket Club, she quickly received permission to lay out a court on an unused portion of the cricket grounds.

Although the game was not an overnight success in America, it was only a few years before every major club in the East had courts. There was little standardization in these early years. With each club having its own rules, conflicts gradually arose. Finally in 1881, an older brother of Mary Outerbridge convened a meeting of the leading New York clubs to bring some order to the confusion. The outcome of this meeting was the establishment of the United States Lawn Tennis Association, which later became the United States Tennis Association.

The first United States championship was held in Newport, Rhode Island, that same year and was won by Richard Sears, who subsequently defended and held his title for the next six years. In 1915, the tournament was permanently moved to the West Side Tennis Club in Forest Hills, Long Island, and was held there through 1977. In 1978, the tournament was moved to Flushing Meadows, New York.

At approximately the same time, another tournament of tremendous importance was being inaugurated at Wimbledon, England. The subsequent elegance and tradition have established this tournament as perhaps the most important tournament in the world.

A few years later in 1884, Wimbledon began its annual tournament for women, and as the ladies gradually began to shed their voluminous clothing, their game became indistinguishable from that of the men.

Boris Becker of West Germany made tennis history in July, 1985, when, at the age of 17, he defeated Kevin Curren in the finals of the men's singles at the prestigious Wimbledon Championships. This made Becker the youngest player ever to win at Wimbledon. He became an instant hero to the tennis world, primarily due to his youth and his excellent court demeanor.

The Davis Cup, one of the most prestigious awards in tennis, was originated by Dwight Davis who, while still a student at Harvard, donated a

The Davis Cup, prestigious award in team tennis

cup to be awarded to the winner of a team match between England and the United States. Today this competition has grown to include teams from all over the world and has contributed greatly to world understanding among tennis players.

INTERNATIONAL TENNIS HALL OF FAME

The Newport Casino was the major site of early tennis in the United States. It is the home of the International Tennis Hall of Fame, which houses a modern pro shop, a shop for tennis memorabilia and a museum of tennis from its early beginnings. Located at the casino is the only "court tennis" court in the United States.

The International Tennis Hall of Fame in Newport, Rhode Island

THE GRAND SLAM

The tennis world recognizes this magnificent achievement as the pinnacle of success. It is very rarely accomplished and has been achieved by very few players. To win the Grand Slam, a player must win the championships of Australia, France, England and the United States in the same season. While several players, including Bjorn Borg, Andre Agassi, and Roger Federer, have come close, only five have been successful. Two were men and three were women. One player succeeded twice.

Date	Player
1938	Don Budge (American)
1943	Maureen Connolly (American)
1962	Rod Laver (Australian)
1969	Rod Laver (Australian)
1970	Margaret Court (Australian)
1988	Steffi Graf (German)

Other tournaments of major importance are:

Davis Cup. Annual national competition with worldwide participation for men. Consists of four singles matches and one doubles match with the first team to three points being the winner.

The Federation Cup. This annual event denotes worldwide competition between women's teams, similar to the Davis Cup. It began in 1963 and has been dominated by Australia and the United States.

Chapter 1: Evaluation

1. What are some of the benefits afforded to players who participate in the game of tennis?

2. How does tennis help to develop honesty?

3. How many calories per hour can be burned by the average tennis player?

4. Briefly trace the origin of tennis.

5. Where was the first U.S. Tennis Championship held?

6. Who was the person who "imported" tennis to the U.S.? From where?

7. What was the origin of the Davis Cup?

8. Define the "Grand Slam."

Equipment and Facilities

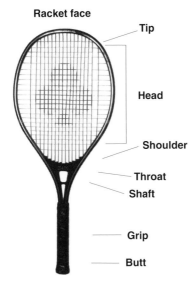

Racket face

Tip

Head

Shoulder

Throat

Shaft

Grip

Butt

Parts of the tennis racket

RACKETS

Tennis racket manufacturing is a fast growing and lucrative enterprise. Only a few years ago, there were but a handful of racket manufacturers charging less than $25 for their best unstrung frames. Now there are many, and the prices have increased nearly tenfold. The tennis industry is constantly marketing new rackets. Multicolored rackets and multi-composition frames of exotic materials are available. The wide-body racket is losing some of its popularity as more variable body rackets are being marketed. What you see today, may not be the "in thing" of tomorrow, nor is there any guarantee that all new changes increase proficiency. Make your equipment selections without worrying about purchasing the most current fads and styles. All rackets, even the most expensive, deteriorate with time, causing loss of power and control; however, the harder substances lose their strength and stiffness more slowly.

QUESTIONS AND ANSWERS

Why do some of the more expensive rackets such as graphite and boron get such poor marks for abrasion resistance?
Many of these so-called miracle fibers wear very quickly. Because of their hardness, they tend to be brittle and chip when striking the court surface. Some manufacturers feature a hard strip of nylon or polyurethane around the outer frame of the racket. Others have developed a replaceable bumper guard for protection. A simple and inexpensive protection in use for years is hospital tape or rubberized electrical tape.

Is flex or flexibility in rackets important?

Very flexible rackets tend to provide more power but less control. A stiffer frame will give a player less power but more control. From a beginner's standpoint, *control* is far more important than speed.

What do the various markings on the handle of my racket mean?

If you have markings, you probably have a quality racket. The numbers and letters themselves indicate the handle size, weight of the frame, and sometimes special model numbers. Handle sizes are indicated by the numbers 4 3/8, 4 1/2, 4 5/8 and 4 3/4. Some recent models use only the numbers 3, 4, 5 and 6 to designate 3/8, 4/8, 5/8 and 6/8. See the chart below.

Racket weight is usually designated by the letters L, M or H immediately following the handle size. The letters indicate a range in ounces and may vary according to the manufacturer.

Markings on racket handle

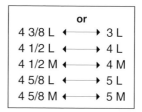

	or	
4 3/8 L	←——→	3 L
4 1/2 L	←——→	4 L
4 1/2 M	←——→	4 M
4 5/8 L	←——→	5 L
4 5/8 M	←——→	5 M

What size and weight racket should I have?

At this point in your tennis career, it is impossible to say with certainty. However, several guidelines may assist you in your initial choice.

If you shake hands with a racket handle, the tip of your thumb should be able to touch the first joint of your middle finger. Also, the average grip size for women is usually 4 3/8 - 4 1/2 and for

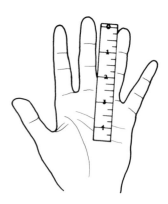

One way to determine handle size is to measure the distance of the ring finger to the long crease in the palm

Selecting the proper racket is an important part of the game

men it is 4 1/2 - 4 5/8. If your hands are unusually large or small for your sex, this would have to be adjusted.

Another widely used method of determining handle size is to measure the distance from the tip of your ring finger to the long crease in the palm, as illustrated in the diagram on page 10.

If your present grip is too large, your arm will probably be tiring very quickly. If the grip is too small, the racket will twist more readily in your hand, making it appear that you are not gripping the handle tightly enough.

How will I know if I need a lighter racket?

Research indicates that for swings of equal speed, the medium-weight racket hits the ball deeper and faster than the light racket. This assumes the rackets are identical except for weight. The best advice is to *pick the heaviest racket that you can handle comfortably.*

Baseliners generally use a head-heavy frame while serve-and-volley players usually prefer a headlight frame. To determine your racket's status, adjust it on a thin balance point until it is perfectly balanced, mark the point, then measure from that point to the tip of the head. If the racket is 27 inches long, the balance point should be 13 1/2 inches. If the balance point is closer to the head, it is head-heavy, and if it is closer to the handle, the racket is headlight.

How do racket materials compare?

The racket materials chart on page 12 may help. Note that the ratings range from 1-8, with 1 being the most or best.

How can a player control the additional power generated by the midsized and oversized rackets?

A player with a wristy, floppy, short swing will have trouble controlling midsized and oversized rackets. To be effective with an oversized racket, try swinging in a smooth, fluid manner and go for a stiffer racket rating. A relatively stiff swing with little wrist usually works best.

What kind of racket would be best for someone with a relatively slow swing?

In general, players having slower swings or compact strokes will benefit from the increased power generated by a stiff-framed racket. Players with faster swing speed generally do better with a more flexible frame.

What is the latest in the "wide body" concept in tennis rackets?

Since 1987 and the Wilson Profile® racket, wide body rackets have tended to decrease in width from approximately 28 millimeters to about 24 millimeters. Players were finding too much power in the originals and were complaining that they were losing ball control and touch. This means they were hitting the ball long and out of the court. Average racket weight also appears to have changed. Ultra-light rackets (under 10 ounces) seem to be on the rise, and anything over 13 ounces is becoming scarce.

What kind of racket should a player use if prone to tennis elbow?

Look for a light racket that is more flexible than average, has cushioned grips and a shock absorbing system. Also, string at the lower end of the recommended tension and with a thinner string.

Racket Materials Chart*

Material	Cost	Strength	Abrasion Resitant	Stiff-ness	Vibration Absorption
Wood	Least Expensive (1)	8	8	8	1
Steel	Inexpensive (2)	6	1	2	6
Aluminum	Inexpensive (3)	7	1	6	6
Titanium	Moderate (4)	5	1	4	6
Fiberglass	Moderate (4)	4	4	7	2
Kevlar	Expensive (5)	3	5	5	3

*Rackets range from 1-8 with one being the most or best according to category.

What are some of the important racket ratings?

Vibration Damping Rating: Indicates how quickly impact vibrations disappear.

Sweet Spot: The point on the racket face giving the least vibrations on ball contact.

Power Zone Rating: This zone is usually located just below the sweet spot center. Balls striking above the power zone tend to lose power as they move nearer the top of the racket.

Overall Stiffness Rating: Indicates "racket feel" to a player. One to four is usually very flexible. Six to ten usually denotes a stiff racket. Stiff rackets typically provide more power and consistency.

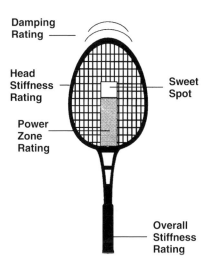

Assuming use of the same material, is there any difference in using a 3/4" grip wrapping as opposed to 1"?

Because the 3/4" grip is narrower, there will be more turns around the handle and less distance between the grooves. Some players believe that more depressions or grooves on the handle give better racket control through reduced slippage. The 1" grip with fewer grooves does seem to be more comfortable. However, it's a matter of personal preference.

What are the advantages of synthetic grips as opposed to leather?

It is generally accepted that moisture is the chief cause of racket slippage. Leather tends to be brittle and lacks moisture absorbent qualities at around 50°F. At 90°F it absorbs well but quickly becomes saturated.

Disposable grip tape

Synthetic wrapping can absorb moisture up to 9 or 10 times better and will give up internal moisture if wiped with a towel. Therefore, many players feel a synthetic grip provides a more secure grip in high, humid temperatures.

Is it possible to clean a sweaty, dirty and slick racket grip?

The racket grip must be clean and slightly tacky for expert performance. Obtain a stiff bristle brush, water and biodegradable soap. Wet the grip, soap it down and scrub thoroughly. Then rinse and allow to dry. Rebrush the dry grip to restore its tack. Many intermediate and advanced players use a disposable grip tape (above) to give better feeling to the handle. Disposable tape gives a secure grip and is easily replaced when soiled.

STRINGS

Racket strings have a self-contained vocabulary. The more important terms follow:

Gauge: This represents the diameter of a string. The thinner the string, the higher the number. An 18 gauge string would be thinner than a 15 or 16 gauge. Generally, the thicker the string the more durable, and the thinner the string the more responsive.

Tensile Strength: This is a measure of overall strength. Synthetic strings range from about 140 pounds to over 220 pounds.

Elongation: This represents the amount of potential stretch in a string. All strings have some stretch, but excessive elongation will produce a sawing action and more wear, plus a lowering in tension. Strings range from about 5% (gut) to 18% (monofilament nylon) with the majority averaging around 10%.

STRINGING YOUR RACKET

It is important to understand some of the principles of deciding to string your racket tighter or looser. **If you string your racket tighter**, the following ideology applies:

- More control
- Less power
- Increased spin
- Reduced durability
- Increased vibration potential for elbow problems
- Decreased sweet spot size
- Decreased string movement

If you choose to string your racket looser, the following ideology applies:

- More power
- Less Control
- Decreased spin
- Increased durability
- Decreased vibration which helps avoid elbow problems
- Increased sweet spot size
- Increased string movement

Stringing a racket

SELECTING A TENNIS STRING

Characteristics of tennis strings affect their playability versus durability. The following applies:

A. Playability String Characteristics
- Softer feel when hitting the ball
- More power and less control
- Often thinner in diameter (the higher the gauge number, the thinner the string)
- Get their better playing characteristics through construction methods or the composition of the material used to make the string
- Tend to lose tension quicker
- Better for elbow problems
- Tend to be more expensive

B. Durability String Characteristics
- Harder "feel" when hitting the ball
- Less power and more control
- Often thicker in diameter
- Get their durability by being thicker or using tough, high-tech materials, or a combination of both
- Hold tension well
- Not suited for elbow problems
- Tend to be more expensive

What are the names of some strings designed to enhance spin?
While most manufacturers make some form of textured string, the following trade names seem to do a good job of enhancing spin: T.O.A. Twister®, Pacific Gear Blend®, Forten Kevlar Gear® and Gamma Rough®.

Should you use the same thickness of string to play on clay or rubico as opposed to a hard surface?
Probably, most players won't know the difference. Soft surface play is much slower, resulting in longer matches, longer points and more wear. Most tournament players and professionals prefer a string one gauge thicker than when playing on a hard surface. Moisture is also associated with soft surfaces, causing increased abrasiveness as both ball and strings pick up gritty particles.

How can I tell if my stringer has done a good job?
There are five basic things to look for:
> **String burns:** If strings are pulled too hard and fast, a grooving or notching effect results. Notching come with normal wear and play, but if made during stringing, will cause premature string breakage.
> **Empty string holes:** All string holes should be filled.
> **Overlaps or crossovers:** Overlapping string at the top of your racket will expose it to all the wear and tear of normal play.
> **Tubing:** Tubing should be used on broken or cracked grommets. Take care that the tubing does not extend more than 1/8 inch above the frame.
> **Uneven weave:** A missed weave pattern indicates sloppy stringing.

What are the best strings to choose to put lots of spin on the ball?
Presently, there is a great deal of experimentation with regard to string shape, gauge and composition. The most important consideration is gauge or thickness. The newest string seems to be a 16 to 17 gauge "micro" string. It is thought that the thinner string creates wider spaces or openings in grid pattern that allow the ball to sink in farther, increasing the "bite" or opportunity for more spin. Low string tension also produces more power and less control, while high string tension provides less power but greater control.

Does string tension influence the velocity (i.e., speed) at which the ball comes off the strings?
Research has shown that when using gut and nylon, ball velocity decreased when string tension was increased from 50 to 65 pounds.

How often should I have my racket restrung?
The amount of spin or cut you impart to the ball usually determines the length of life for your strings. There are, however, two general rules on restringing. One is to restring as many times in a year as you play in a week. The other is to restring after every 30 hours of hard play.

Is there a difference between synthetic gut and nylon?
Synthetic gut is actually a nylon blend and essentially is a marketing term for
the more expensive nylon strings.

**I am hitting my shots long. Is there anything that might help me in terms
of stringing my racket?**
Most experts would suggest raising your string tension by 2-4 pounds.

REDUCING "TENNIS ELBOW"

Tennis elbow is a name given to describe a sore elbow that develops
when playing tennis or doing some other activity with your dominant arm. It is
generally considered a strain of a ligament or cartilage in the elbow area, and
can be reduced dramatically if the following suggestions are understood:
- Select a string designed to help elbow problems
- String at a lower tension
- Add lead tape to increase stability and sweet spot area
- Increase the size of your grip if it is too small
- Install a shock absorbing grip
- Install a vibration dampener in your strings
- Use a large head racket
- Select a racket with a grip system designed to reduce shock and vibration
- Select a more flexible racket
- Get a good warm up of the entire body, with special emphasis on the
  shoulders
- See page 168 for additional information

TENNIS BALLS

Basically there are four different kinds of tennis balls: regular, heavy duty,
pressureless and high altitude. Regular balls contain more wool in the covering,
thus making a tighter nap so as to pick up less dirt. Heavy duty balls are made
for hard abrasive surfaces and have substances such as nylon and dacron in
the covering. Since there is no appreciable pressure within pressureless balls,
they are able to last until the ball core loses it resiliency. They seem to feel
heavy and have a peculiar sound when hit, thus, they are not popular in the
United States. High altitude balls contain less air pressure within the ball so
as to equalize the atmospheric conditions of being at a higher elevation.

When choosing tennis balls, it is best to stay with name brands.

What kind of tennis balls should I buy?

Choose name brand tennis balls. Costs usually range from $2 to $4 per can of three. Players who play on firm abrasive surfaces such as rough concrete or asphalt will realize some savings if they purchase only heavy-duty balls, which have an extra heavy covering of felt. Tennis ball quality is determined by standardized requirements, and manufacturers who meet this standard will display a "USTA Approved" stamp on their merchandise.

Most manufacturers inflate their balls with compressed air or gas and pack them in pressurized containers. A pronounced hissing sound when opening a new can indicates that the pressure has been maintained. Once opened, balls rapidly lose their resiliency. Should you open a can and not hear this sound, return your purchase. Most retailers will gladly exchange the can. Any ball that cracks or breaks early in play should also be returned for replacement. A set of opened balls can quickly be checked by squeezing for firmness and dropping for bounce. Any ball that appears unusually soft or does not bounce at least knee high has probably lost its compression. Heavily worn balls become unduly light, and some balls that become shaggy in wear tend to collect moisture during play, thus becoming very "heavy" and slow. Even new, unopened tennis balls that have been stored for several months lose some of their vitality.

How are tennis balls made?

Tennis balls are two half-spheres of rubber bonded together and covered with glued fabric. These hourglass-shaped pieces of fabric contain combinations of nylon, dacron, wool and cotton depending upon the specifications of a particular manufacturer.

Most balls made in the U.S. are pressurized by placing the two halves inside a heated pressure chamber. They are then bonded together, and when removed, the ball has acquired the pressure of the chamber. Other manufacturers achieve pressurization by inserting small amounts of water and a vaporized chemical into the halves. Then the rubber core is sealed and heated causing the chemical to pressurize the interior of the ball. The approximate interval pressure is 11-14 pounds per square inch.

What about balls that are advertised as pressureless?

These balls have a thicker and more bouncy core than pressurized balls. While they have a heavier feel and do not bounce quite as high, they are less influenced by climate and last longer than regular pressurized balls.

How long can tennis balls be kept in a sealed can?

Recent technology has drastically reduced the number of cans that lose their pressure even though they have an unbroken seal. The average shelf life of a sealed can of pressurized balls is 6 months to 1 year.

Should I buy regular or extra heavy tennis balls?

The type of tennis balls you choose depends upon the court surface you play on. The basic difference is the nap, or cover. Heavy duty balls fluff up more quickly and this helps to protect the cover against abrasive wear. Regular balls have a tighter nap so as to not pick up as much grit or particles. Heavily fluffed balls tend to pick up moisture quickly, thus making them heavier and slowing the pace of a game.

TENNIS SHOES

Tennis shoes are probably the most important part of any tennis player's wardrobe. If you play on any soft surface, such as clay or rubico, you must have smooth-soled sneakers. Basketball or jogging shoes are unsuitable, since their soles are too deeply indented and leave court marks. If you play on a very hard surface you should have cushioned insoles for better comfort. Leather-topped shoes offer a little additional support but tend to cause more sweating, since they do not "breathe." Leather shoes are also more expensive.

Tennis socks are equally important, because they can easily affect the condition of your feet. Socks should be a mixture of cotton and wool and have excellent absorbent qualities. Many tennis players always wear two pairs of socks to facilitate this.

Are polyurethane soled shoes better than rubber soled shoes?

Urethane shoes are lighter than rubber and, in some cases, may wear longer than rubber. However, there seems to be a correlation between slipperiness and durability— the more durable the more slippery, particularly in late night or early morning play.

Must I buy special clothing to play tennis?

This depends on where you play. Many private clubs have

Proper tennis shoes are important

strict written and unwritten rules governing the court dress. Whether you wear a pair of basketball or track shorts rather than tennis shorts, however, is not going to influence the quality of your game unless you feel self-conscious. It is important that you wear light-colored comfortable, absorbent clothing and a head covering if playing in intense heat.

A MODERN COLLEGIATE FACILITY

The pictures on the following pages are of the University of Florida's Ring Tennis Complex and are located on the campus. There are a total of 15 courts, including three covered courts for use in inclement weather. The home of the Men's and Women's teams, the facility has offices for the coaches of both teams, and includes well equipped locker rooms for each team, a training room, comfortable conference area, storage facilities and a racket stringing area. Each stadium court (facing the bleachers) has an umpire's stand, benches, and an electric scoreboard, along with complete enclosure of windbreakers. Also, video equipment with camera and recorder have recently been added to each court, enabling matches to be put on tape for follow-up critique. The stadium will hold over 1,000 spectators. All are hard courts for ease of maintenance.

In 1999 the facility won the USTA Outstanding Tennis Facility Award, and the City of Gainesville presented the tennis facility the "Excellence in Institutional Facility Award". Also, in 2001 it was presented the Athletic Business Conference "Facility of Merit Award".

University of Florida's Ring Tennis Complex

TENNIS COURTS

While tennis court dimensions are standardized by the governing agencies of tennis, court composition and court settings are varied. In general, types of courts will be determined by climate and area of the country. Most good courts, however, will be laid out on a north-south line to minimize sun problems and will usually be fenced and surrounded by large hedges and/or a green plastic saran windbreaker to decrease the effects of wind and to increase ball visibility.

Soft Courts

The South has a higher proportion of soft courts than any other area of the United States. The most common materials are clay, rubico and Har-tru®. Soft courts are easy on the feet and legs. The style of play is slower and the ball tends to "sit up" more. Soft courts favor a soft hitter and diminish the attacking player's game.

The primary disadvantage of soft surfaces is the difficulty of keeping them in good playing condition. They must be swept, watered and rolled daily. A freezing climate will cause the court lines to pull out of the ground, and should players use a recently thawed or very wet court, damage can easily occur that might take weeks to repair. Some porous types, however, do have the advantage of quickly absorbing a hard summer shower and being ready for play in less than an hour.

Pictured are three indoor courts at the Ring Tennis Center.

Hard Courts

Hard courts of asphalt, composition materials and cement are more common in the U.S. than in other parts of the world. The Western states emphasize this type of court. The surface requires little upkeep and provides a uniform ball bounce and increased visibility.

The primary disadvantage of hard surfaces is the wear on a player's feet, legs and shoes. The pace of play is much faster, since the ball rebounds quickly from this surface, favoring the driving hitter and server. Hard court surfaces, can be modified by the contractor to provide slow, medium or fast play.

Nets and Accessories

Tennis nets are usually made of synthetic materials such as nylon or polyethylene to restrict the effects of moisture. Manufacturers using cotton or natural fibers dip their nets in a creosote-tar substance to retard the rotting process. Metal nets, while durable, have a tendency to bow in or out, creating inaccuracies in measurements for net height and distance from the net to the baseline. Center straps are necessary on all but metal nets since it is very difficult to achieve a fine adjustment with the windlass on the net post.

Measuring for proper height

Standard Dimensions of a Tennis Court

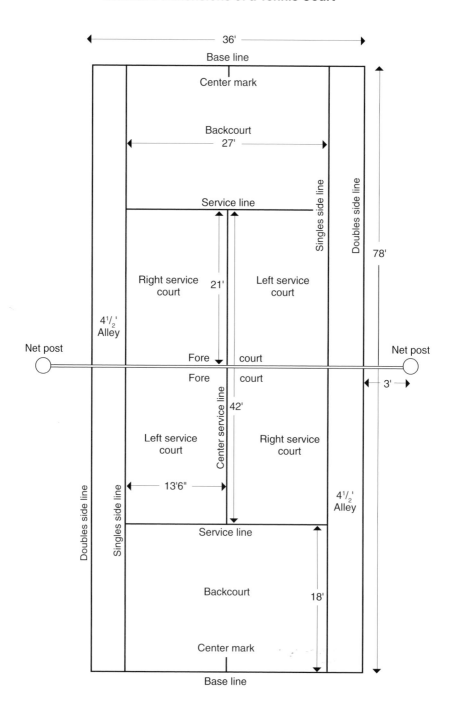

Chapter 2: Evaluation

1. Quote at least one method of determining proper racket handle size.

2. Discuss the pros and cons of hard vs. soft tennis courts.

3. When selecting the weight of your tennis racket, what is the general rule used?

4. Discuss the advantages of loose vs. tight strings and thin vs. thick strings.

5. Diagram a tennis court, naming all lines and areas.

6. Why should a player generally hit the ball over the center of the net?

7. Contrast heavy duty tennis balls as opposed to regular tennis balls.

8. What should a player look for when buying tennis clothing?

9. Diagram the parts of a tennis racket.

10. State at least one method used for determining how often a tennis racket should be restrung.

11. What is the average size racket grip and weight for both women and men?

Chapter 3
Scoring and Playing the Game

Tennis rules are usually written in technical language and specific points are often hard to find when needed. In addition, a number of unwritten rules, while not specifically covered in the rules book, are nonetheless very important to the game. See the Appendix for the complete Rules of Tennis.

QUESTIONS AND ANSWERS

The following questions and points of procedure seem to be the most relevant and are most asked by beginners.

What is a game and how do I keep score?
The points are:

No points or 0	= Love
One point	= 15
Two points	= 30
Three points	= 40
Four points	= game (if two points ahead of opponent)

If the players' scores are even after six or more points in a game, the score is referred to as deuce. Should the server go ahead by one point after deuce the score becomes "advantage server" or "ad in," and should the server win the next point, it is "game." However, if the score is tied after six or more points and the receiver wins the next point after deuce, then the score becomes "advantage receiver" or "ad out." If the receiver wins the next point it becomes his or her "game."

What is a set?
A set is a part of a match that is completed when a person or team wins at least six games and is ahead by at least two games. For example, the score might be 6-1, 6-2, 7-5, 8-6, etc.

Units of Scoring

points $\longrightarrow$ games $\longrightarrow$ sets $\longrightarrow$ match

What is a tiebreaker?

The tiebreaker is a fairly recent innovation used to complete a set when the game score becomes 6-6. This prevents long, drawn-out contests which may be detrimental to players.

The 9-point Tiebreaker

At the present time, the 9-point tiebreaker is rarely used; however, it is included for your information. In the tiebreaker, the first player to obtain five points wins the set.

Singles: In singles, if player A is due to serve the next regular game, A serves two points as in normal play, starting from the right side. Then the serve goes to the other side with player B doing the same. After these four points the players change sides and the service again goes to player A, who serves the next two points. If a winner has not yet been determined the serve again goes to player B, and B serves two points. At this time, should the score be tied four-all, player B serves point nine. However, A, who is the receiver, may elect to receive the serve from either the right or left service court. The players do not change courts after the set and player B begins serving the first game of the new set.

Doubles: Assume team A-B is playing team C-D: A and C serve the first four points, sides are changed, and B and D serve the next four. Should a ninth point be necessary, player D serves the third serve. Players must serve from the same side from which they have been serving.

The 12-point Tiebreaker

The 12-point tiebreaker has become the most popular tiebreaker used today. Normally in the U.S. this tiebreaker—or any tiebreaker—takes effect when the set score reaches 6-all. Also, the International Tennis Federation (ITF) description indicates that the tiebreaker normally would not be used in the third or fifth sets of a best of three or best of five match, but any nation has the option of stipulating, in a given tournament, that the tie-breaker will be in effect even in those identifiable final sets of matches. In the 12-point tiebreaker, the first player or doubles team to reach seven points and be two points ahead of the opponent will win the set.

Singles: A serves first point from right court; B serves points 2 and 3 (left and right); A serves points 4 and 5 (left and right); B serves point 6 (left) and after they change ends, point 7 (right); A serves points 8 and 9 (left and right); B serves point 10 and 11 (left and right), and A serves point 12 (left). If points reach 6-all, players change ends and continue as before. A serves point 13 (right); B serves points 14 and 15 (left and right); etc., until one player establishes a margin of two points. Players change ends for one game to start the next set, with player B to serve first.

Doubles: Follow the same pattern, with partners preserving the sequence of their serving turn. Assuming A-B vs C-D: Player A serves first point (right); C serves points 2 and 3 (left and right); B serves points 4 and 5 (left and right); D serves point 6 (left) and after teams change ends, point 7 (right). A serves points 8 and 9 (left and right); C serves points 10 and 11 (left and right), and B serves point 12 (left). If points reach 6-all, teams change ends and continue as before—B serves point 13 (right); D serves points 14 and 15 (left and right); etc., until one team establishes a margin of two points. Teams change ends for one game to start the next set. A tiebreaker game counts as one game in reckoning time between ball changes.

ALTERNATIVE SCORING METHODS

With today's competition for time in everyone's active schedule, there has been a push for alternative scoring in tennis. Some of these **include Short Sets, Best of Two Matches, and Match Tiebreaks.** They are explained as follows:

Short Sets are simply a shortened version of a normal set. Instead of the first player to win six games, a player only needs to win four games. At three games all a 12 point tiebreaker is implemented. If players split short sets, a Match Tiebreak is used in lieu of a third set.

Best of Two Matches consists of a competition where two normal sets are played to determine the winner. A player winning both sets is considered the winner of the match. If players split sets (winning one set each), a Match Tiebreak is used in lieu of a third set.

Match Tiebreaks are played in the same procedure as a 12 point set tiebreak. The difference is that a player must reach 10 points (versus 7 points) and win by a two point margin.

These alternative scoring methods help competitors play matches in short time frames and enable greater use of court time when availability is limited. It also helps greatly in attracting spectator groups when potentially lengthy matches are regulated to end a predictable time.

VASSS "No-Ad" Scoring[1]

A player need win only four points to win a game with the no-ad procedure. That is, if the score goes to 3 points-all (or deuce) the next point decides the game. It is game point for both players. The receiver has the right to choose to which court the service is to be delivered on the seventh point.

---

[1]VASSS (Van Alen Simplified Scoring System). James H. Van Alen established the Tennis Hall of Fame at Newport, Rhode Island Casino in 1954. In 1969 the USTA adopted "sudden death" scoring, and used it in the 1970 U.S. Championship at Forest Hills.

If a no-ad set reaches 6 games-all, a tiebreaker shall be used which normally would be the 5-of-9. However, in collegiate tennis, the 12-point tiebreaker is used. **NOTE:** The score-calling may be either in the conventional terms or in simple numbers; i.e., "zero, one, two, three, game." The latter is usually preferred.

Then who wins the contest or match?
Most competitive matches are determined by whoever wins two of the three sets. However, some prestigious matches and tournaments are determined by the best three out of five sets.

Are balls that hit the boundary line good? Yes.

What is a let serve and how many times can a person have a let serve?
A serve that hits the top of the net and falls into the proper service area is a let. There is no limit to the number of let serves a player may have.

What if a ball other than a serve hits the top of the net and falls into my opponents court?
It is a good shot on your part and must be returned by your opponent.

If I make a poor toss on the serve, can I catch the ball rather than trying to hit it?
Yes, but it is a fault if you swing and miss.

What if my opponent allows the ball from a previous point to remain on his court, and I hit the ball during a succeeding rally?
It is a great shot and your point if the correct ball is not returned.

Can I throw my racket at the ball and hit it? No.

My doubles partner has a weak serve and I am getting killed trying to play the net. What should I do?
Back up to the baseline, at least on all second serves.

My partner does not see well and returns serves that are frequently faults. Is it legal for me to call serves directed to him, out?
Yes, it is your responsibility.

In doubles, can the best serving partner serve first at the beginning of each set?
Yes, this is generally a good idea unless the sun or wind causes unusual problems for your partner.

What is a pro-set?

A pro-set is one in which a person or team wins at least eight games and is ahead by at least two games. Example: 8-0; 8-1; 8-2 etc. It is used as an official scoring for NCAA competitive tennis.

Who keeps score?

Players usually keep their own score. Other than some tournaments in which the umpire will call out the score, it is usually the server's responsibility to call out the score.

Can a player touch the net or reach over the net to hit the ball?

A player may not touch the net while play is in progress and may not reach over the net unless the ball has first bounced on her side and then been carried back across by the wind or severe backspin.

Who serves first in a match? It is customary to flip a coin or spin the racket. The winner has the choice of serving or receiving, or the choice of court. The loser has the remaining choice.

What if a ball rolls across my court when a point is being played?

A let or replay is in order if it is immediately called out. Do not wait until you see if you win or lose the point before calling "let."

Can I serve the ball underhanded? Yes.

Can I have some rest in a two out of three set match?

No. This has been discontinued in both men's and women's competition.

What is a foot fault?

The most common type of foot fault occurs when the server makes contact on or within the baseline before hitting the ball. The offending player loses the opportunity to put the ball in play. See Rule #8 in the Appendix.

Foot fault

Do players ever change ends of the court?
Yes, at the completion of games 1, 3, 5, 7, 9, etc., in each set, and in the case of tiebreakers.

What happens if I allow a ball to hit me or I catch it while I am outside of the court?
This is technically illegal and must be considered a good shot for your opponent even though it is obviously an out shot. Always let the ball go to prevent hassles.

Can I yell or deliberately distract my opponent like I do in basketball and football?
No.

What if I blink just as my opponent's shot hits the court and I am not sure whether it is in or out?
Always give your opponent the benefit of the doubt. Do not play the ball and then call it out. Remember that each player is responsible for calling out balls on his or her side of the court.

What if I am forced to leave the court entirely to return a shot, and hit the shot around the net post rather than directly over the net?
If the ball lands in your opponent's court you have made a fine shot.

What if the ball just barely touches me during a point?
You lose the point.

What if you are playing someone who is obviously cheating you?
The best solution is to not play with the person; however, you could request an umpire if it is a tournament match or ask for a replay of a certain point.

After playing a very long first match in a tournament, the tournament director allowed me only 15 minutes to rest before my second match. Is this legal?
Unfortunately, yes. The usual practice, however, is to not require a person to play more than one match in the morning and one in the afternoon. Chapter 13 provides information on conditioning for extended play.

How much time is allowed to change ends of the court between games?
Technically, one and a half minutes. However, most people do not complain if you towel off, take a drink and wipe your glasses. Opponents may complain if you repair your racket or change socks and shirt.

I occasionally play indoors and my opponent's lobs sometimes hit the lights because of a low ceiling. He always insists on replaying the point. Is this legal?
If a shot hits an obstruction, whoever hits the ball last loses the point.

In doubles, can my partner and I change sides of the court to receive a serve?
No. You must wait until the beginning of a new set.

My opponent frequently "quick serves" me. What can I do?
Quick serving is illegal. However, if you swing at the ball it is assumed you were ready. Do not swing at the ball; tell your opponent that you were not ready.

One of my opponents is better than I am and she always wants to rally to see who serves first. If I were better than you and could get you to agree to this, I would too. Tell her the rules say to either spin or flip for choice of serve.

Spinning the racket for choice of serve—up or down?

My opponent always wants to begin play on the "first serve in." Is this legal?
No. All practice serves must be made before the first point is played.

My opponent hit an out shot that stuck in the net under the strap, just below the top. He claimed he should have a replay because his topspin would have taken the ball over. I gave him another shot, but I think I was taken. Was I?
Yes. Rule 17 says that a ball embedded in the net is out of play and the hitter loses the point.

Can I serve the ball underhanded with lots of spin? Yes.

Can I fake the underhand serve and then serve overhand?
Yes. There are no restrictions on preliminary motion once the receiver is ready for your serve.

Do I have the right to request that my opponent remove a ball lying in his court?
Yes, but at the appropriate time.

I play pretty well, but when the match goes into a tiebreaker, I can't seem to win. Any advice?

Every tiebreaker point is a key point. In a regular game you can get fancy or reckless occasionally and if it doesn't work you still have time to retrench. The tie break simply does not allow much room for a recovery, once you fall behind. Hit your high percentage shots and "hang in there." You will be surprised how many of your opponents will fold if you just keep the pressure on. The ability to do this, however, requires a high level of body conditioning and willpower. A weakness in either or both of these areas could be your problem.

Points of Player and Spectator Etiquette

1. Before beginning, always introduce yourself to your partner and opponents. Shake hands with players after the match.

2. Always check net height at the beginning of a match. One convenient way is to take two standard rackets and stand one end with the head of the other on top.

3. Take all practice serves before playing any points.

4. As a server, do not begin serving any point unless you have two balls at the ready.

5. Observe the foot fault.

6. Call lets and faults out in a loud clear voice. A point of the finger upward or sideward will also reinforce a voice call.

7. Never "quick serve" an opponent.

8. Never give unsolicited advice and restrict comments to the conduct of the game.

9. Control emotions and temper.

10. If your ball rolls onto an adjacent court, wait until the point is over then shout, "Thank you, please?"

11. When returning a ball to players on another court, wait until their point is finished and they are looking at you.

12. Return only served balls that are good.

13. Do not make excuses. If you lose, you lose, and always shake hands with your opponent.

Points of Player and Spectator Etiquette, *cont.*

14. Do not lean on the net to retrieve a ball.
15. If you must cross an occupied court to reach yours, wait until their point or game has been completed; then go quickly to your court.
16. Hit any shot requested by your opponent during the warm-up period.
17. Call a let whenever another ball enters your court and return it to its owner.
18. Keep score accurately.
19. Give the benefit of the doubt on close calls to your opponent.
20. Be on time for your match.
21. Dress properly according to local customs.
22. Announce the score when you are serving.
23. Never "boo" a player.
24. Applaud good shots.
25. No moving while ball is in play (spectators).
26. No loud talking or yelling when ball is in play.
27. If spectating, allow the umpire or players to call the match. They are in a much better position than you to call most shots.
28. Do not ask a spectator whether or not a shot was in or out.
29. Never hit a ball directly at an opponent except during official time in play.
30. Never monopolize the courts.
31. Never wear basketball or jogging shoes when playing tennis.

TENNIS TERMS

Ace: A serve that is hit beyond the reach of one's opponent.

Ad: A shortened word for advantage which refers to the next point after the score is deuce.

Ad in: The score when a serving player wins the next point following deuce.

Ad out: The score when the receiving player wins the next point following deuce.

Advantage: The next point after deuce.

All: Denotes a tie score as in 30-all, meaning 30-30.

Alley: A 4 1/2 foot lane on both sides of the singles court and necessary for doubles play.

American twist: A type of topspin serve used mainly in doubles play. The topspin imparts a high bounce allowing the server more time to follow the serve to the net.

Approach shot: The shot taken just before the hitter moves into the net.

ATP Tour: A series of tournaments for professional men players.

Australian doubles: A formation in which the net person lines up on the same side as the server.

Backcourt: The court area between the service line and the baseline.

Baseline: The back line or the farthest line from the net.

Baseline game: One who rarely attempts to take the net or play in the forecourt.

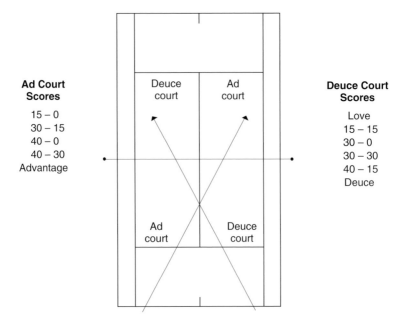

Big game: A style of play popularized by Jack Kramer and utilizing the hard serve, followed by a pressing net attack.

Carry: An illegal shot causing the ball to be slung or hit twice before crossing the net.

Center mark: A short perpendicular line that divides the baseline at its center.

Chop: A downward stroke of the racket, usually causing the ball to rise slightly and, depending on the surface, to skid or bounce low.

Closed tournament: An event open only to the members of a particular club or geographical area.

Continental grip: A grip utilizing a position halfway between an Eastern forehand and classic backhand. The grip does not require a player to change grips for the forehand and backhand stroke.

Crosscourt shot: When the ball is hit diagonally from one side of the court to the opposite corner on the other side.

Default: When a match is awarded to one player because of non-appearance or if one player is unable to continue a match.

Deuce: A 40-40 tie score and anytime thereafter in the same game when the score is even.

Deuce court: The right service court viewed from one's own baseline.

Dink: A softly hit ball, usually intended to keep the ball in play.

Double fault: Failure to put both the first and second ball of one's serve into play.

Doubles: Match play between two teams of two players each. Mixed doubles involves having a man and woman on each team.

Down the line: A shot moving parallel to the sideline.

Drop shot: A lightly hit ball, usually having backspin and designed to barely clear the net with minimum force.

Eastern grip: Most used grip for hitting forehand shots. Also called the "shake hands grip."

Fast court: A smooth court surface causing the tennis ball to move quickly to the hitter.

Fault: The failure to serve a ball into the proper service court.

Foot fault: An illegal serve caused by the server stepping into the court as the racket makes contact with the ball.

Game: One portion of a set that occurs when one person or team wins four points and is at least two points ahead. On tie games, such as 30-30 or 40-40, it is the first side to gain a two-point lead.

Grand Slam: A tennis achievement requiring the winning of the U.S. Open, the French Open, the Australian Open, and the Wimbledon Championships all in the same year.

Ground stroke: A forehand or backhand stroke occurring after the ball has bounced.

Hacker: A tennis player with limited form and skills.

Half volley: A defensive shot usually occurring when the ball is hit halfway between a volley and a regular ground stroke. The ball is blocked or hit with a very short backswing just as it begins to rise from a bounce.

Invitational tournament: Competition open only to players who receive the invitation.

ITF: The International Lawn Tennis Federation.

Let: Whenever a point needs to be replayed. Generally it occurs when a serve hits the top of the net and lands in the proper service area.

Let serve: As above, but pertains only to the service.

Lob: A high soft shot used to drive one's opponent back to the baseline, or to allow the hitter more time to assume better court position.

Love: Zero in tennis scoring.

Match: Any tennis contest—singles, doubles or teams.

Match point: The final point needed to close out a match.

Net umpire: When officials are employed, this person calls let serves.

No or **out:** The terms used by some players to denote a ball that did not land within the proper court area.

No ad scoring: A new version of scoring requiring the winner to have four points. If the score is tied at 3–all, then the next point determines the winner.

No man's land: The court area located between the baseline and the service line; generally considered to be a poor area to attack from or to defend.

Overhead: A free swinging hard shot usually very much like the serve.

Passing shot: A ball hit low and hard to the side of a person who has moved in to "take the net."

Poach: Generally refers to the doubles play of a net person who is able to pick off shots intended for a partner.

Pro set: An abbreviated match that is completed when one player wins at least eight games and is ahead by at least two games.

Pusher: A soft hitter who is generally very steady.

Rally: An exchange of shots after the serve, usually from the baseline.

Receiver: The person who is to receive and return the serve.

Retriever: A type of player who plays a defensive game and returns all shots.

Service break: The loss of a game by a server or a serving team.

Service line: A line running parallel to and 21 feet from the net.

Set: A component part of a match that occurs when a player or side has won at least six games and is ahead by at least two games.

Slice: To hit the ball with sidespin and/or a slight undercutting motion.

Slow court: A rough or soft surface court causing the tennis ball to "bite in" or to move more slowly to the hitter. Good examples of slow courts are clay and rubico (Har-tru®).

Split sets: When both players or teams have won one set each and the match outcome will be determined by the remaining set.

Straight sets: To win a match without losing a set.

Sudden death: When a tiebreaker goes to the final point.

Sweet spot: The point on the racket face giving the least vibrations on ball contact.

Take two: Whenever the receiver indicates that the server should repeat two serves.

USTA: United States Tennis Association.

VASSS: The Van Alen Simplified Scoring System. A set is completed whenever one person scores 21 or 31 points. It is rarely used today.

Volley: A short backswing shot taken before the ball hits the court. The primary weapon for doubles play.

Western grip: A forehand grip that allows the hitter to impart severe topspin to the ball.

WTA Tour: A series of tournaments for professional women tennis players.

A. Scoring Problem for a Game

Point No.	A	B	Score
1	●		
2	●		
3		●	
4	●		
5		●	
6		●	
7	●		
8		●	
9		●	
10		●	

A = Server
B = Receiver

B. Scoring Problem for a 12-point Tiebreaker

Point No.	A	B	Score
1	●		
2		●	
3		●	
4	●		
5		●	
6	●		
7	●		
8		●	
9		●	
10	●		
11		●	
12	●		
13	●		
14		●	
15	●		
16	●		

A is the first server and serves from the south side of the court.

Questions for Scoring Problem B

1. How many points were served by A? By B?

2. What was the final score in the set?

3. What was the final score in the tiebreaker?

4. To which court was the 9th point served, right or left?

5. To which court was the 14th point served, right or left?

6. When the game was concluded, was the server serving from the north or south side of the court?

7. How many times did the players change ends of the court?

8. Which players will be serving the first point of the next set?

Chapter 3: Evaluation

1. What are your choices when you flip a coin for first serve?

2. If a ball merely nicks a line, is it considered a "good shot"?

3. What does the term "sudden death" in a tiebreaker mean?

4. During a regular set, when do you change ends of court?

5. The score is 30-15, which court does the server use for the next point?

6. The returned shot was clearly going to land out of my court by at least six feet; however, I was standing within my court and caught the ball at a point over my head. Whose point is it?

7. Who serves the first game of the next set following a 9-point tiebreaker? A 12-point tiebreaker?

8. List several ways you can lose a point other than not returning it back across the net.

9. List the points in a game, using correct scoring terminology.

10. Can you ever reach across the net to hit a ball? Explain.

Gripping the Racket

HITTING THE TENNIS BALL

Since most of you have probably received elementary tennis instruction and have played some tennis prior to reading this book, you know that the forehand drive is the "bread and butter" shot of the game. It is likely that, since this stroke seems easier to hit than the backhand, you favor the shot and find yourself playing three-quarters of the court with the forehand. You worry that your opponent may hit the ball down the line on the backhand side.

If this is the case, do not be concerned, since you must have a good forehand, and the only way to acquire one is to practice hitting from that side. However, you must begin to hit a greater percentage of backhand shots; otherwise, the difference in the ability to hit both shots will appreciate even more, and you will become more vulnerable.

As with any endeavor, there are certain generalizations or principles which, if applied, will improve performance. This does not rule out individual differences, but if one studies the professionals in tennis, most seem to have nearly identical form in their basic strokes.

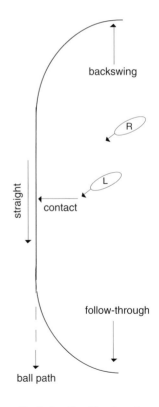

Racket path of forehand stroke (top view)

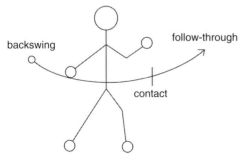

Racket path of forehand stroke (side view)

FOREHAND GRIP

Eastern Grip

The Eastern grip is the most commonly used grip. It is often called the "shake hands" grip, since the racket handle is grasped as you would the hand of a friend.

The palm will be in the same plane as the face of the racket, and the heel of the hand will rest lightly against the butt of the handle. The fingers should be spread with the index finger spread slightly more than the others. This will cause a "V" (the junction of the thumb and index finger) to rest squarely on the top of the handle so that if a line were to be drawn from the "V" it would fall over the right shoulder.

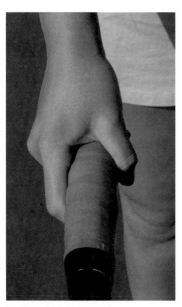

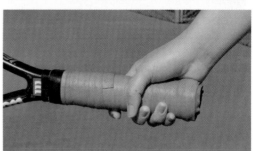

Eastern Forehand Grip

Continental Grip

The Continental grip places the hand midway between the Eastern forehand and the Eastern backhand. The advantage is that no change has to be made for forehand or backhand shots. Therefore, this grip is sometimes favored by those who react slowly at the net, volley a great deal, and/or play doubles exclusively. The disadvantages are a slight reduction in hitting power and the necessity of a strong wrist.

To assume the Continental grip, move your hand around the handle to the left of the Eastern grip. The knuckle of your index finger will rest halfway between the top of the handle (as in the classic backhand) and the back of the handle (as in the Eastern forehand). Finger spread and thumb position is the same as the Eastern forehand.

Side view

Top view

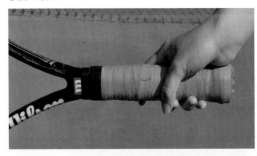
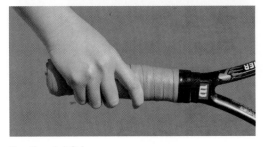
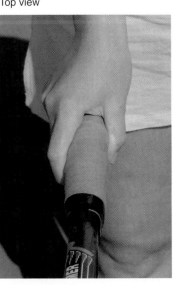

Continental Grip

Western Grip

For the Western grip, move the hand in a clockwise direction from the Eastern grip so that more of the palm of the hand will be under the handle rather than behind it. The racket hand rotates a quarter of a turn toward the bottom (clockwise) of the handle. This creates a closed racket face, more or less depending on the extent of the rotation.

Due to the publicity given topspin by professionals, this grip is becoming more popular, as it permits exaggerated topspin to be placed on the ball. Younger players, however, have difficulty with the low trajectory caused by this grip. A player must learn to adjust to an aiming point much higher than the Eastern forehand in order to clear the net.

The change from forehand grip to backhand grip can be difficult. Because of the exaggerated turning of the hand in the Western forehand grip, the distance to the Eastern backhand is lengthy. In a fast exchange, there may not be enough time to make the change. The Western grip is not recommended for beginners.

Western Grip

Top view

Rear view

Semi-Western Forehand Grip

The Semi-Western Forehand Grip can be best described as a grip between the Eastern Forehand and the Western Forehand Grips. This grip allows for top spin with power and is ideal for passing shots. Although it is difficult to hit low balls because the racket face is closed, it is ideal for balls struck above the waist. Semi-Western Grips allow for increased racket head speed and, therefore, it becomes easier to disguise the direction of your shots. On slower court surfaces where the ball bounces higher, you will find this grip is the grip of choice.

"Extended" Western Grip

An "extended" western type (author's name for it) has become a very popular grip with many top players today. The advent of accelerated top spin has created a new grip technique over the past ten years. Players who use this grip hit with a very aggressive upward swing and, along with a new racket face coming into contact with the ball, the effect is a severe degree of top spin being imparted on the ball. The stance is basically an "open" one in that the footwork and shoulders are more 'square' to the net when compared to the eastern or traditional western strokes.

In the extended grip, the racket face becomes parallel with the court rather than perpendicular to it (see diagram). The contact with the ball is on the lower or underside of the racket. When one is accustomed to seeing the standard grip used, this new technique looks quite unusual. However, the results are amazing. One should be advised that this takes a tremendous amount of practice as it runs against traditional stroking techniques. The authors have been amazed at how hard the ball may be hit using this technique - and still remain well within the court. It is becoming very popular in collegiate and professional circles.

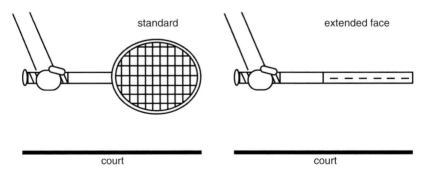

Extended Western Grip

BACKHAND GRIP

Eastern Backhand Grip

One of the most common faults among beginners is the attempt to hit backhand shots using a forehand grip (without turning the racket). This makes it impossible to present the racket face perpendicularly to the ball and at the same time maintain a smooth fluid stroke.

To place the racket face in the desired position, turn the hand a quarter turn counterclockwise from the Eastern forehand grip. This will place the index finger knuckle **on top of the handle.** The thumb should be kept at a diagonal, but may be shifted upward slightly for additional support. Fingers should be spread slightly as in the Eastern forehand. Turn the racket by simultaneously loosening the forehand grip and turning the throat of the racket with the left thumb and index finger. This should be done as the left hand is guiding the racket back into a full backswing.

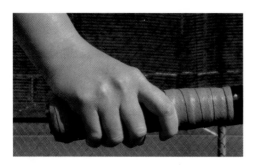 

Eastern Backhand

Two-Handed Backhand Grip

In the last several years, a number of ranking tennis players have demonstrated that the two-handed backhand can be a very effective weapon. Its advantages are that it allows a person to hit with more power and control the racket more effectively, especially if the person is very small or weak. The two-handed grip also provides more opportunity to hit with topspin. Its chief disadvantage is that a player cannot reach as far on wide shots as with the conventional backhand. This can, however, be overcome with good footwork.

> **Common Backhand Grip Errors**
>
> - Failure to change from the forehand grip.
> - Improper placement of the thumb or forefinger.
> - Insecure grip at moment of impact.
> - Leading the stroke with the wrist or elbow.
> - Not having a firm wrist.

To assume the two-handed backhand grip, place your right hand in the same position as for the Eastern backhand. The left hand is placed in a position similar to the Eastern forehand, but just above and touching the right hand. Both hands should be placed on the grip at the beginning of the pivot turn and preparatory to the backswing.

The left hand plays the dominant role with the right providing control and support. Ball contact should occur as the ball reaches the front foot.

Two-Handed Backhand

Many of today's players utilize a forehand grip that is unlike any of the standard grips of yesterday. The reasoning behind the development of this grip lies in the desire to accomplish two elements:

1. To hit the ball hard and
2. To keep it within the boundaries of the opponent's side of the net.

Traditional grips limit greatly the force used in striking the ball. The CONTINENTAL grip will lift the ball, causing it to sail out of bounds when hit hard, while the EASTERN grip, although lowing the trajectory still creates problems in keeping the ball in bounds. The WESTERN grip closes the racket face to the ball, creating a necessary upward swing into the ball to create topspin to pull the ball down into the opponents court. This can be done hitting the ball very hard or less so, but counting on the amount of topspin to pull the ball into the opponents court. Thus, the three faces appear as illustrated on page 53 at contact.

"Extended" Western (Forehand) Grip

The "EXTENDED" WESTERN grip places the palm of the racket hand along the side of the racket (see picture). Thus, the face of the racket is parallel to the ground. The hitting area of the racket is facing the ground. As the ball approaches, the player drops the racket head and swings upward through the ball with a great deal of power causing severe lift, which is countered by tremendous spin, and power. The ball is struck very forcefully to create sufficient lift and topspin. It is a very powerful stroke and weapon when executed properly. This technique is seen in countless players, utilizing all types of courts and competitions.

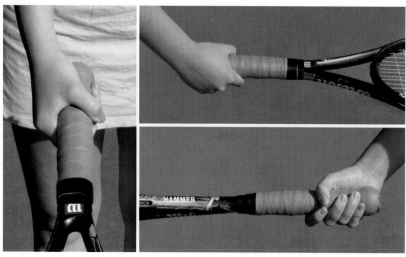

"Extended" Western Grip

Continental: the racket face is open

Eastern: the racket face is flat

Western: the racket face is closed

Relationship of the racket face to each type of grip

Chapter 4: Evaluation

1. In tennis, what one factor probably causes more missed shots?

2. When an opponent hits the tennis ball toward you, what are the four most important evaluations that must be made?

3. The basic Eastern forehand imparts what kind of spin to the ball?

4. Rank the following components of tennis as to importance and defend your ranking: hitting power, player speed, spin and accuracy.

5. The basic Continental backhand, moving in a high to low trajectory, develops what type of spin?

6. Why should you cease body movement just momentarily before striking the ball?

7. What is meant by "stroke preparation," and why is it important?

8. List several problems or mistakes that frequently cause errors among beginning tennis players.

Principles of Stroking

Simplicity

Most everyone has heard the story of the man who was to deliver an important speech. His wife, while typing the speech, made a notation at the top of the page. The notation was "KISS," with an arrow drawn to the bottom of the page. At the bottom of the page were the words, "Keep it simple, stupid." So, the first principle of hitting the tennis ball is to "keep the stroke simple."

A fairly good player once swung at a tennis ball and hit himself in the mouth with his own tennis racket. The end result was eight stitches. Obviously his stroke was not a simple stroke. The tennis swing is not a complicated windup with fancy gyrations. Rather it is a smooth, nearly effortless and fluid motion, causing the head of the racket to increase momentum, culminating on impact so that the total power of the swing is transferred into the tennis ball. One way to help develop this fluid swing is to stand in front of a mirror and simply "dry swing" your tennis racket while thinking of the various components of a good stroke.

Early preparation is an essential. Most teaching professionals believe that if those many unnecessary movements that tend to creep into a tennis stroke can be eliminated, the player will be rewarded by success.

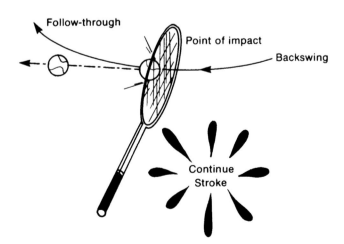

To begin hitting a forehand, just turn your shoulder to begin your backswing and keep your racket slightly lower than the intended contact point. Many beginners make the mistake of just moving the arm back in their backswing. The shoulder rotation is the key ingredient in keeping the swing smooth and simple.

The tennis stroke is basically a low to high trajectory. The purpose of the low to high stroke technique is that it allows the player to stroke the ball with sufficient height to clear the net, thus avoiding the cause of most errors. To use the stroke, drop the head of the racket to a point slightly lower than, but in line with, the anticipated contact point of the ball. Don't add anything fancy to this backswing motion—just take the racket back. As the ball approaches, simply swing the racket into the ball, raising the racket into the follow-through. No excess motion of the feet, wrist or arm is needed.

Many of us believe that we have to do something extraordinary to be successful. In tennis, the opposite is true. The more unnecessary motions that are eliminated, the better.

Concentration

This principle, probably more than any other, separates the winners from the losers in tennis. When hitting the shot, concentrate almost entirely on watching the tennis ball. The majority of missed shots in tennis occur when the player makes a shot while not totally watching the ball. This results in hitting the ball off-center. Remember, aim the ball from the **center** of the racket.

The principle also applies to other sports. Ted Williams, the famous baseball hitter, said that he always tried to follow the baseball with his eyes from the pitcher's hand to the moment of impact with his bat. One way to develop stroke concentration is to never look up until after hitting the tennis ball. How often have you looked to see what your opponent was doing just as you were about to hit the ball?

Eliminate Unnecessary Motion

It is difficult to hit a moving target while moving your own body too. However, if you stop, even momentarily, you will notice an improvement in accuracy. Beginning tennis players will improve their stroking ability if they cease moving just prior to hitting the ball. Beginning players also frequently and unnecessarily bend at the knees and hips, so that in addition to unnecessary lateral motion, they bob up and down with the stroke. Many beginners loop their swing instead of bringing the racket back more in a straight line. If you are having trouble hitting the ball, try repeating to yourself just prior to stroking the shot, **"Straight back—step swing."** At the same time, bring the racket hand back in a straight line at the expected bounce level (height) for the shot being played.

Develop Smoothness of Motion

Do not be discouraged if you feel awkward the first few times you attempt a new stroke or new movement. Repetition will increase your smoothness and ultimately your movements will become as "smooth as silk."

Control

A beginner's primary goal should be consistency and accuracy rather than speed or spin. To develop the "feel or touch" necessary for consistency, concentrate on hitting the ball with only moderate pace. In time, you will gain confidence in your strokes and will want to gradually increase the pace of your shots.

The angle of the racket face at the moment of impact determines the ball spin. The basic spin is a slight topspin created by starting the shot low and finishing high, thus causing the ball to spin in a forward motion and resulting in a downward drop or curve in the flight of the ball.

Concentration and control are essential.

Balance and Power

Balance is fundamental to all sports and tennis is not an exception. The ability to handle low shots and to move quickly in any direction necessitates that a player be relaxed and stand with the knees slightly flexed. Power is the force that is gained by the fine coordination of racket, arm and weight transfer necessary to move the ball in the chosen direction.

Early preparation is essential. Just as in softball where the batter steps into the pitch, the tennis player should step into the line of the shot. This is accomplished by transferring body weight to the forward stepping foot, which is kept on the ground. The heel of the back foot is usually off the ground and bears little weight. The face of the racket then moves into and through the intended flight path of the ball. Additional power and a free swing will be possible if the waist is kept relatively straight. However, remember that an increase in power can contribute to loss of control, so proceed with caution.

Preparation

Success in tennis depends upon all of the aforementioned qualities. An understanding of them and a ready application enhance the chances of winning and playing well. Perfecting these qualities will demand many hours on the court, practicing both mentally and physically.

Preparation is that additional ingredient that turns the difficult shot into an easy one. When the opponent hits the ball, there are several things to evaluate and little time to do it. They are:

- the speed of the ball (slow, medium, fast)
- the type of spin you have to contend with (topspin or backspin)
- the height of the ball (shallow or deep)
- the angle of the flight (close or wide)

Quick adjustment to these factors will show itself in the ability to return the ball successfully. Ideally, be ready to return the ball by the time the incoming ball strikes your court. This **preparation** will mean moving quickly to the ball and allowing sufficient time for the footwork and stroking sequences to occur. There is no substitute for early and proper preparation. Anticipation is the key. With serious effort, your game and success in stroking can improve rapidly.

Watch the Ball

Both beginner and experienced players must watch the ball. All players get distracted at times, and fail to concentrate on this key element of the game. You can't hit what you don't see. Try to watch the ball all the way to your strings. This assures a stroke that contacts the ball correctly, and in the center of the sweet spot of your racket. Try it—it works!

Chapter 5: Evaluation

1. Define the following words and explain why each is important: spin, speed, control, accuracy and power.

2. Beginning from the ready position, describe the simplicity of a tennis stroke.

3. Most stroking errors are caused by one simple and easy to correct technique. What is it?

4. The basic stroking technique imparts what kind of ball spin?

5. What does the word "preparation" mean to the game of tennis?

6. Why is it important to cease body movement just prior to executing a tennis stroke?

7. Your opponent hits the tennis ball toward you. List four things that you must quickly evaluate.

8. How can a player anticipate where the opponent will hit the ball? What are some of the telltale signs?

Chapter 6
Basic Footwork Patterns

Each stroke, whether it be a forehand or backhand, is very similar to the one preceding. The only difference is that the strokes are made in different places. This is why footwork is important. It is essential to be able to move fluently and in a relaxed, controlled manner. Of all the skills needed to reach a successful and satisfying level of tennis, footwork is one of the most important. It has been said that footwork is 50 to 70 percent of the game. While the percentages can be debated, it is certain that footwork is vital to the game and cannot be overlooked or taken lightly. When observing a good player, it is easy to see the relationship between footwork, stroke production and success.

Many inexperienced players hit the ball in all sorts of positions. Most of these are uncomfortable, and the results are frequently unsatisfactory. Good footwork makes a difficult job easy. As stated earlier, most strokes follow the same basic technique—forehands are stroked about the same way each time, with slight adjustments. Backhands, volleys, etc., are the same. The difference in forehands may frequently be in footwork preparation.

The following explanations of proper footwork patterns will progress from simple to complex.

THE READY POSITION

As a player learns the game of tennis, it becomes obvious that tennis balls cross the net at various speeds, angles and heights. It is infrequent that two shots are the same, so there is an immediate need to be continuously prepared, expecting everything. It may be necessary to move quickly in any direction, covering half the court either on the forehand side or the backhand side. On the other hand, you may have to move very little, except to step forward and contact the ball. Alertness is the key! The ready position is the stance used to facilitate quick movements. That is to say, the player can move in any direction, quickly and totally under control, whether the move is one step or a series of steps.

In the ready position, the racket is held comfortably, usually with an Eastern forehand grip. The other hand supports the racket, holding it loosely at the throat. The arms are close in to the body, holding the racket in front of the upper torso. Elbows are relatively close to the chest. The waist is slightly bent, allowing the body to bend forward, indicating readiness. Knees are slightly flexed, with the weight evenly distributed on the balls of the feet. Feet are about shoulder-width apart. Comfort is the keynote. In advanced tennis, the player receiving the service may jump slightly, anticipating the contact of the ball on the server's racket. This gives the receiver a "quick start" to position for the return.

Ready position

THE FORWARD PIVOT
(To be used for balls close to the body—one step away.)

This footwork pattern may be achieved in three ways, each one correct and proper in its own style. Each style accomplishes the procedure of turning the body sideways to the net, allowing the racket to flow into the backswing. If completed properly, each style allows the player to step into the stroke, thereby creating a weight shift into the ball. The three variations are explained in detail.

The cross step pivot: This variation begins with the ready position. As the ball approaches the player, the player pivots on the ball of the right foot and steps across and slightly forward with the left foot. As the ball approaches the contact area, a slight weight shift is made as the racket moves into the ball. Upon the completion of the stroke, the weight is on the forward foot. The rear foot remains stationary. The toes are in contact with the ground, but the heel will be slightly raised. This footwork pattern will remain the same for both the forehand and backhand stroke.

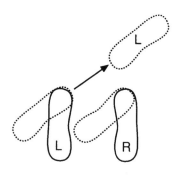

Cross Step Pivot

The turn and step pivot: This variation involves two separate movements by the player. As the ball approaches, the player merely turns the body to the side. There is no distinct footwork pattern, but a cross step may be used as discussed on the previous page. However, the forward foot will line up with the rear foot in a position approximately parallel to the net. The feet are kept close together. As the ball approaches, the player steps into the ball at a 45° angle, shifting the weight into the stroke as contact is made. The follow-through remains the same as in the cross step pivot.

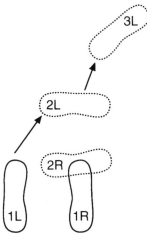

Turn and Step Pivot

Turn and Step Pivot

The twist and step pivot: The third variation is similar to, yet quite different from the other pivot procedures. The player, upon seeing the ball approach, turns sideways to the net, pivoting the feet to the side from the ready position. As the ball approaches, the foot closer to the net steps at a 45° angle into the ball as the forward swing is initiated.

The follow-through for this pivot, as in the others described above, remains the same. The weight is forward at the completion of the stroke. In all three variations the recovery to the ready position simply involves stepping back with the forward foot, again facing the net and assuming the ready position.

These three footwork patterns will include many variations among players. Basically, however, the user will find that these three patterns will more than suffice for stroking forehands and backhands with proper form. **It should be noted that these same patterns are used with the backhand.**

THE REVERSE PIVOT

The reverse pivot is used when the ball is coming either directly to the body or so close that using a forward pivot would crowd the stroke. To properly position oneself for this stroke, begin with the basic ready position as shown in page 64. The following pattern is used for the right-handed hitter.

With feet in the ready position, begin with a slight crouching movement in the knees. Start as soon as the flight of the ball is determined. With the weight evenly distributed on the balls of both feet, pivot on the left foot, turning the body to face the forehand side as you step. Position the feet as shown in the illustration. Having positioned yourself, put your weight once again on the right (rear) foot. You are now in a position very similar to those mentioned earlier under the forehand pivot.

As the ball approaches the contact area, with the weight comfortably on the rear foot, execute a forward step into the ball, as was done with the basic forward pivot. Simply explained, you have just stepped back and away from a ball coming in too close to the body and have placed yourself in a position to comfortably reach the ball and execute the stroke.

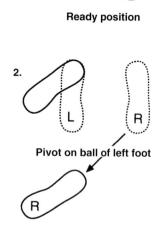

1.

Ready position

2.

Pivot on ball of left foot

Step back with right foot

The reverse pivot is identical for the forehand and the backhand. The player will benefit by starting early in preparing for the stroke.

Reverse pivot series

THE SIDE-SKIP OR SHUFFLE STEP

This footwork pattern is used when the ball is away from the body—not close enough to be reached by a simple forward pivot. The side-skip pattern is a comfortable, easy movement that allows the body to pivot into the ball without breaking the flowing, rhythmical motion.

As with the other footwork patterns, the starting position is the ready position. When the opponent hits the ball, the footwork pattern should begin. This promptness is necessary because of the distance one must travel to get into position and is complicated by the speed, depth and spin to the ball.

When moving to the right side, the first step is with the right foot. Initially, the player assumes a slight crouch, and the weight is moved by pushing with the ball of the left foot and stepping with the right foot to the side. The step should cover about three feet or a distance comfortable for the player. When the right foot comes in contact with the court, the left foot follows and comes into place alongside, thus completing the first "step" of the side-skip pattern.

This pattern continues until the player is one skip or step away from the desirable pivot point. As the final step is made, the player begins a forward pivot into the ball, as explained earlier in the chapter. This means that on the last step, the right foot contacts the court and a pivot is made, pointing the right toe at a 45° angle to the net. As the weight is taken on the right foot, the left foot begins the step-across into the ball, continuing the 45° angle mentioned above. As the stroke is made, the weight will be maintained in the pattern outlined and no additional steps will be needed, except to recover into a ready position. However, this movement is used to take the player away from the "home" position on the court, usually to the corners. It will be necessary to reverse it again to recover back to the center of the baseline (backcourt) area for the next stroke.

In moving to a ball that is either short in the court or deep, pushing the player back away from the baseline, a short side step motion is used. Short, quick steps are used rather than longer ones, as some adjustment will be necessary due to the low or high bounce. A player can improve the situation by maintaining an alert, intense attitude. This will create a quicker initial response to each shot.

Every player must frequently run to reach the ball. This happens when the player is too far from the ball and cannot otherwise reach the shot. However, upon reaching the ball, adjustments are necessary to create proper stroke footwork.

Footwork Tips

- Keep a close watch on the ball to insure an early "jump" on the incoming shot. Begin your preparation as soon as the ball leaves the opponent's racket.

- Anticipate where your opponent will hit each shot and begin moving.

- Look at the possible angles of return—to your right and left—now recover to the center of this angle.

- When you contact the ball and return it to your opponent, recover quickly, as soon as your follow-through is completed.

- To gain maximum benefit from the footwork pattern, movement into the stroke should be rhythmical, relaxed, comfortable and early.

- Be in position with racket cocked in the backswing no later than the bounce of the incoming ball.

- As you execute your stroke, keep the rear foot in place only allowing the weight to shift forward to the other foot. Do not step with the rear foot as the stroke is made.

- Upon completion of your stroke, don't waste valuable time watching the shot, recover immediately.

- Think constantly about proper footwork procedures and movements. This will help you become more alert to the ball and your movement patterns.

- Use a shuffle or side-step pattern to recover to your home position as this will be helpful in both preparation for the next stroke and in preventing the next ball from going "behind" you.

Chapter 6: Evaluation

1. Why is footwork so important in tennis?

2. Describe the ready position.

3. List six footwork tips.

4. Demonstrate the following: Cross step pivot; turn and step pivot; reverse pivot and the side skip.

5. Why do most receivers of service jiggle their body slightly or bounce just before the server strikes the ball?

6. What is the purpose of the reverse pivot?

The Forehand

HITTING THE FOREHAND

Since the Eastern grip, the ready position and footwork have been discussed, we are now ready to proceed to a discussion of stroking fundamentals for the forehand drive.

Backswing

As soon as it becomes clear that the ball will land on the forehand side, the backswing is started. Beginners will experience more success by drawing the racket back in a straight line until the head of the racket points directly at the fence behind the baseline. This is accomplished by turning the left shoulder and moving toward the ball so that when the ball arrives, the early backswing allows time to adjust to unusual spin, speed or bad bounce. As you acquire more experience, you will probably loop the racket head slightly in the form of an egg-shaped half arc.

The backswing

The forehand stroke

At the point of full backswing, the racket head should be just slightly below the point where the ball will be hit. This is a low to high swing, which is necessary for imparting a slight topspin to the ball and for clearing the net. For low bouncing shots, bend the knees and drop the shoulder farthest from the net. This will keep the racket head from dropping below the handle and is necessary for maintaining control.

In the forehand stroke, the backswing does not utilize a straight arm or a locked elbow. The backswing is a relaxed comfortable reach behind the body, with the elbow about six to eight inches from the chest. The wrist is back to allow for a proper face on the ball at contact.

Pivot and Movement of Feet

In the beginning position, the feet are approximately shoulder-width apart, standing in the center of the court and one to three feet behind the baseline. As you move toward the ball and stop at the desired position, weight should be on the rear foot. The next movement is a step into the ball, much as a softball hitter does when stepping into a pitch. This transfers the weight into the line of shot and provides the power necessary for a successful stroke.

Additional points of importance are:
- Stand straight from the waist up.
- The front knee should never be stiff.
- The toe of your back foot will be in contact with the ground, but the heel will be off the ground.

Impact point

Impact Point

Whenever possible, hit the ball at waist level, since this is the easiest and most effective point of impact. Should the ball be lower than waist level, lower the racket arm by bending the knees and not the back.

As your weight transfers to the front foot and the racket head moves toward the impact point, attempt to make contact with the ball slightly in advance of the front foot and beyond the midpoint of your body.

Follow-Through

Follow-through is as important to tennis as it is to basketball shooting, football throwing or any other athletic endeavor involving hand-eye coordination. Perhaps the easiest way to develop follow-through is to establish checkpoints in your swing which, if adhered to, will guarantee that follow-through is taking place.

Follow-through checkpoints:

1. At the completion of your forward swing, is your front knee slightly bent with the ball of your foot in contact with the court?
2. Is the heel of your other foot (the back leg) slightly off the court at the conclusion of the swing?
3. Did you start the backswing low and finish in a high position—well out in front of your body and at least eye high?
4. Are you standing tall from the waist at the end of your follow-through?
5. Is the racket face still standing on edge at the end of your forward swing?
6. At the completion of your swing, are you looking over your elbow and forearm to where you want the ball to go?

Follow-through

When hitting the forehand, try to think of the racket as being an extension of your arm. Try using your arm and racket as if you are sweeping a full table of dishes onto the floor in one full motion. Remember to relax your grip between shots, otherwise the muscles of your arm, hand and wrist will experience early fatigue.

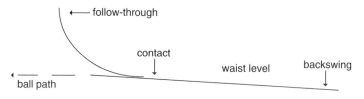

Forehand Groundstroke Path

Due to the improved technology of today's rackets, the game style of tennis has changed. Racket technology has allowed for increased power when generating ball pace and that translates into faster rallies and less recovery time. To compensate for less time, there has been a move to hitting tennis strokes with an open stance. For right handed players on the forehand side, instead of stepping with your left foot toward the ball, the right leg carries the weight (called "loading"). This open stance allows for a quick recovery to the center of the court. It should be noted that preparing with shoulder rotation and the upper half of the body is required for hitting a forehand with a closed or open stance. Also, players hitting with this open stance will predominately use either a Semi-Western or Full Western grip.

HITTING WITH TOPSPIN

Recent television coverage of tennis has shown that top professionals use topspin with a high degree of success. This has created a desire by many players to develop topspin for both forehand and backhand shots. To determine whether this method of stroking the ball is best for you, first examine the advantages and disadvantages before making a valid decision.

Advantages

- Topspin causes the ball to drop quickly to the court after clearing the net.
- The trajectory of a topspin drive usually clears the net with greater height and results in fewer net errors.
- When returning a ball against a player at the net, the ball, if hit with a lower trajectory, dips quickly and causes the opponent to return the ball upward.
- When used with proper depth, the opponent must either stroke the ball on the rise or back up to stroke the ball. Most players, unless highly advanced, have difficulty doing this.
- A high topspin drive aimed toward the opponent's backhand creates a high bouncing shot and causes a very difficult return.
- You can create better angles since the ball can drop quickly after clearing the net.

Topspin stroke series

follow through

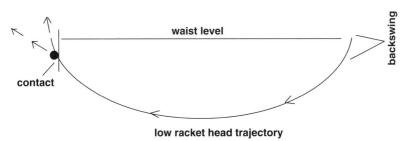

Disadvantages
- The player usually changes from the Eastern grip to the Western, causing an unfamiliar face on the racket.
- The footwork pattern changes, causing the player to open the stance for the topspin drive.
- The exaggerated low-to-high arm movement may contribute to arm and shoulder problems.
- Many hours of practice are necessary.

A common problem in changing to the topspin stroke will be the immediate lack of control in directing the stroke. This is due mainly to the new angle of the racket face. The closed face of the Western grip will cause many balls to be hit into the net. To counter this problem, the player must adjust the aiming point of the stroke into a higher level above the net.

Grip
Since most topspin players will use the Western grip, or a modification, a quick review of Chapter 4 should help to refresh your memory of the grip. Remember to turn your hand one quarter turn underneath the handle from the standard Eastern grip to the Western grip.

Footwork
The footwork technique will change slightly, in that your stance will allow you to stroke upward on the ball more aggressively to create the topspin. Some players stand facing the net when contacting the ball and have excellent results.

A right handed hitter will keep the right leg outside, creating an open stance with his weight transferring from the right leg before contact to the left leg after contact.

Hitting the Ball
As the ball approaches, the first thing you do in preparation is to rotate your shoulders so that your non-hitting shoulder is facing the net. Notice that you do not have to bring your hitting arm back any farther. The swing is a loop, with the wrist dropping the racket head below the ball before contact. **It is very important to move the contact point in front of your body** with a Western grip and the wrist will create the topspin by creating more racket head speed as you swing at the ball. Notice how the shoulders will rotate fully back to facing the net after contact.

The follow-through continues upward to a point slightly past the height of the player's head. Recovery to a ready position must be quickly made to prepare for the next return.

COMMON FOREHAND PROBLEMS

Hitting the balls long.

Consistently hitting balls long may mean your opponent is hitting the ball hard. Use the opponent's speed by shortening your backswing and letting the ball ricochet off your racket. Another possibility is that the face of your racket is open or tilted too far up, or you may be allowing the ball to descend too far on the bounce before hitting. Try to take the ball at its highest point of bounce and bring the racket head back on a higher plane. Another common cause of hitting long is that the stroke is aimed too high to keep the ball within the lines.

Hitting short or weak shots.

The lack of hitting power usually results when a player does not step into the ball and does not shift weight with each shot. Check for proper follow-through and make sure the racket head finishes well in front of the body. Delaying the swing and allowing the ball to get past may also cause this problem. Move the impact point forward. Late hits are sometimes caused because the backswing is delayed. Remember to **hit through the ball.**

Hitting shots consistently to the right (right-handers) or to the left (left-handers).

It is likely that either the feet are lined up improperly or the swing is late. Practice hurrying the backswing and try to move the impact point in front of the midpoint of the body.

Hitting the ball consistently to the left or "pulling the ball."

Hitting too soon may be the cause. Not moving the feet into proper footwork positions is also a frequent reason to pull the ball to the left or right.

Ball always seems to land right at your feet.

The old axiom is "all the way up or all the way back, but not in between." The area between the back service line and the baseline is called "no man's land" and is a poor place to be caught.

Balls go in all directions with no set pattern.

Try setting up more quickly. This means "hustle." Other problems are looking at your opponent instead of the ball and hitting with a loose wrist. Try to maintain a firm wrist and do not try to hit either a racquetball, table tennis or badminton shot. Good tennis, more than any of these other sports, requires a firm wrist. Proper timing is also helpful.

Hitting the ball off center.

Watch the ball more closely. Failure to watch the ball into the racket causes the ball to occasionally hit on the frame of the racket or on the side of the face. Prepare early and watch the ball to correct the problem.

Forehand Checklist

Using another player to rally with your partner, circle the appropriate letter as you observe your partner demonstrate his/her ability to use the forehand stroke. Allow appropriate warm-up time to determine accuracy in your observations.

Ratings: G = Good, F = Fair, P = Poor

G   F   P   1. Player uses the correct grip or a slight variation.

G   F   P   2. Anticipation is good, allowing sufficient time to move to the ball.

G   F   P   3. Proper footwork is used on the court.

G   F   P   4. Footwork is efficient—no wasted steps.

G   F   P   5. Player steps into the ball with the right foot as contact is made.

G   F   P   6. Backswing is taken back early and not rushed.

G   F   P   7. Topspin and/or slice is used effectively during the stroke.

G   F   P   8. Racket swing is relatively level into the in-coming ball—low to high.

G   F   P   9. Contact with the ball is made in front of the left foot.

G   F   P   10. There is little or no wrist evident in the stroke.

G   F   P   11. The follow-through begins immediately as contact is made.

G   F   P   12. The follow-through flows smoothly to the completion of the stroke.

G   F   P   13. The racket head is high and in front of the left shoulder at finish.

G   F   P   14. Recovery is rapid, awaiting the next shot.

Comments: (use reverse side if needed)

Forehand Evaluation Comments:

Chapter 7: Evaluation

1. What are the three recommended grips for the forehand stroke?

2. Why is the Eastern forehand the easiest stroke to learn?

3. Why is the follow-through so important to the Eastern forehand stroke?

4. What is the usual cause of weak shots or balls that bounce short?

5. List the advantages of stroking the ball with topspin. What are the disadvantages?

6. Why should you "cock" or lay the wrist back just prior to the forehand stroke?

7. Trace a line showing the directional flow of the racket head during the forehand stroke.

8. Explain the importance of footwork when hitting the forehand.

Chapter 8

The Backhand

To many people, the backhand is the most difficult stroke in tennis. To others, it is the strongest stroke. The difference is probably in the player's dedication and determination to learn the fundamentals of the backhand and to practice enough to groove the shot.

Due to the necessary grip change, the backhand sometimes feels insecure, giving the player a sense of weakness. Understanding the proper technique of the stroke helps to overcome these fears and allowing enough practice time builds confidence.

Changing the Grip

The Eastern forehand grip, used by the vast majority of players, is the most comfortable grip. It is easy to understand why it is so popular. The shake hands grip is easy to assume, comfortable to hold and blends well with the physics of technique. It is not a proper grip for the backhand, however, because it is necessary when hitting a backhand stroke to change the angle of the racket face.

The grip change from the Eastern forehand to the Eastern backhand involves a rotation of the hand one quarter turn counterclockwise (to the left) on the handle. The following checkpoints indicate that the rotation has been done correctly:

- The racket face becomes flat, allowing more hitting area for the ball.
- The "V" formed by the thumb and forefinger is on the top of the left bevel on the handle.
- The large knuckle of the forefinger is on top of the top forward bevel of the handle.
- The fingers remain spread to allow more control along the entire racket handle.
- The palm of the hand, if opened, faces down toward the ground.
- The thumb comfortably lies alongside the handle, diagonally across the rear facet—not with the "thumbprint" on the facet.

The backhand stroke:
ready position,
backswing, contact
point, follow-through

Wrist action should be kept to an **absolute minimum** when performing this stroke. The less wrist the better. Although this grip is initially less comfortable, constant use generates a positive attitude toward the change and a vast improvement in the game.

The change from the forehand to the backhand grip usually occurs as the ball is traveling toward the player. Most players in the ready position use a forehand grip while waiting for the ball. As the ball approaches toward the backhand, however, the change becomes necessary. While moving the body for proper stroke alignment, change from the forehand to backhand grip, supporting the racket with the other hand at the throat. Finish high!

Backswing

As the ball approaches, the body is moving into position using proper footwork procedures. When the body begins to turn to the side, the grip change should be completed. Usually a player will keep both hands on the racket—one on the handle and one supporting the racket along the throat during the backswing.

The backswing—waist (hip) high

Ideally, the swing should be timed so that the ball is hit between the knee and the waist—in the general area of the hip or thigh. The back-swing should be taken back at the same height as the anticipated contact point—hip high.

As the racket is taken back, the racket arm tends to straighten, allowing the handle to stay down at the level of contact. That is, the racket hand is down below the waist. The support arm, along the throat of the handle, is also kept relatively straight. This causes the racket to remain parallel to the ground throughout the backswing and the face of the racket to remain perpendicular to the court.

The length of the backswing will differ depending on the speed of the incoming ball and the quickness of the player. Usually a full backswing is desirable, taking the racket back just past a line of 180° or perpendicular to the net.

The wrist is firm throughout the entire backswing procedure and the grip is tight along the handle of the racket. Caution should be used to maintain a **level** backswing. The player should not lift the racket head or drop it downward as the initial backswing movement is started. The racket should be taken back on a plane level with the anticipated contact area. Remember, the ball will come at various heights, causing some backswing movements on a low level and others at a high level. Fortunately, most are in the center of the extremes. The basic keys to success are (1) watch the ball closely and (2) start backswing preparation early.

Contact Area

When hitting a ball using the backhand stroke, the ball contacts the racket six to eight inches in front of the forward foot. That is to say, at contact, the racket is further toward the net than in the forehand.

As the ball approaches, the racket begins its forward motion toward the ball. The hand tightens on the racket handle and the arm becomes firmer as the forward motion of the racket continues. It is necessary to make the wrist as strong as possible to absorb the impact of the ball.

For a successful stroke, be certain that the head flow of the racket leads the way into the ball. In other words, that it does not trail the wrist and arm action moving forward. Rather, the arm, wrist and racket flow as one smooth pattern in a straight path. The major strength for the movement pattern is from the shoulder.

Keep the shoulders level with the court throughout the entire stroke. This will eliminate the common error of raising the shoulder of the racket arm on contact, causing the ball to fly on an upward trajectory and frequently to go out of bounds.

As the motion flows from the backswing into contact, a concentrated effort should be made to keep the stroke parallel to the court. The level path of the racket will allow maximum head contact with the ball, providing a drive that goes relatively deep into the opponent's court. It will also create a slight amount of topspin to bring the ball down on the court.

The contact point is six to eight inches in front of the body.

Since the contact point is being made six to eight inches in front of the body, maximum use can be made of the forward shift of weight into the ball. However, care must be observed to keep from lifting the ball. As the racket meets the ball, the hitter should drive through the ball to establish a definite drive pattern—usually four to six inches will suffice.

Follow-Through

The follow-through is the guidance system for the stroke. For example, if the follow-through is low, the ball will stay low. If it is straight, the ball does not clear the net, but usually will hit near the net cord.

Proper follow-through is a smooth upward flow of the racket that begins after the ball has made contact. Please note that sufficient upward movement should be started, however, while the racket is on the approach to the ball—or contact area. The follow-through lifts the ball over the net in the direction the racket is aiming. When swinging from low to high, the following hold true.

Follow-through

Low follow-through: Ball stays low (into the net).

Level follow-through: Ball stays at the same height.

High follow-through: Ball goes over the net.

This works, of course, if other things are also done correctly.

The direction of the ball is determined by the direction of the racket head at contact. If the desired flight is crosscourt, then the upward motion of the racket head is crosscourt. If you desire the ball to go down the line, then the upward motion is down the line. This is the basic pattern for aiming the ball, and it works.

The player should note that the wrist is kept firm throughout the follow-through and the racket arm is kept straight to give proper guidance to the ball. This greatly aids in controlling the stroke.

Two-Handed Backhand

The two-handed backhand is probably the latest innovation in tennis. Although it is not new, the two-handed stroke has become very popular. This may be due to the fantastic successes of most of the world's leading players. Another reason for the trend is that youngsters learning the game will definitely have a problem using one hand for the backhand. At the early stages of development, the wrist, grip and arm are not strong enough to adequately control the racket upon impact with the ball, thus the two-handed stroke is necessary. A strong two-handed backhand is a very good offensive weapon.

Although there are reach limitations in this stroke, proper footwork overcomes the problem. The player using a two-handed stroke should be conscious of developing proper footwork patterns and the necessity of using them for each stroke. There is no substitute for good footwork.

When using a two-handed backhand, there is a distinction between which hand becomes your dominant hand. If you are a right-handed player and your bottom hand is using an Eastern Backhand grip, then your bottom hand becomes the dominant hand and is the primary hand used to generate the

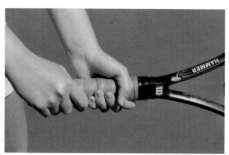

Continental grip   Semi-Western grip

stroke. If your bottom hand is in Eastern Forehand grip or Semi-Western grip, then your top hand becomes the primary hand. An advantage of using an Eastern Forehand or Semi-Western grip as the bottom hand is that a player does not have to change the bottom hand when hitting off the forehand side, and therefore saves time.

The player may experiment with either of these two; however, the grip illustrated above seems to be the most comfortable. Another benefit to this grip is that as a young player's strength develops, there may be a desire to learn a one-hand stroke. If so, the proper grip will have already been learned.

Basic techniques for the stroke follow the normal patterns explained earlier. To achieve consistency, accuracy and pace, early preparation and proper footwork combined with the appropriate backswing, level stroke and fluid follow-through, are essential. Dedicated practice will be the keynote to success.

One thing is certain—the two-handed backhand is here to stay! There are too many world class players using it to be otherwise. Below are listed the advantages and disadvantages of using this stroke.

Advantages	Disadvantages
+ Provides more topspin and power	− Less reach than the one hand
+ Better for baseline players	− Demands more exact footwork
+ Provides powerful service returns	− Difficult to slice or chop ball for backspin
+ Better suited for younger and/or weaker player	

COMMON BACKHAND ERRORS

Contacting the ball late—behind the forward foot.

Begin preparation earlier, as soon as the ball leaves opponent's racket. Watch the ball closely. Anticipate the probable direction of the ball. Have racket back at full backswing position by the time the ball bounces.

Too much wrist used.

As the pivot is made, tighten the grip on the handle, straighten the arm, and strengthen the wrist. Begin forward movement early, leading with the racket head. This is done by turning the entire arm into the stroke.

Leading with the wrist or elbow.

This common error is corrected by mentally preparing early for the stroke and concentrating on allowing the racket head to lead the way into the hit. Stroke with the shoulder and weight shift rather than just an arm and wrist movement. Keep the arm, wrist, hand and racket in a straight line as the stroke is made.

Trajectory is too low.

Follow-through is low or begins too late. As soon as the hit is made in front of the body bring the racket head up sharply into the desired direction.

| Ready position | Full backswing | Step into the ball |

Trajectory is too high.

Too much wrist used in the stroke, thereby accelerating the racket head as contact is made or the ball is hit, the shoulder is lifted upward, causing the flight of the ball to angle up. A high trajectory can also be caused by opening the face of the racket as contact is made. Correction is made by closing the racket face somewhat.

Too much topspin.

Improper face on the racket (closed) at contact or the trajectory of the forward movement of the racket into the hit is improper. This is usually caused by either dropping the racket head initially or swinging upward at a sharp angle into the ball. Wrist becomes a problem here also. Level out the stroke as explained earlier, and correct the racket face.

Ball pulls to the right (crosscourt) excessively.

Caused primarily by poor footwork. Adjust stance and timing. Contact ball six to eight inches in front of body. Allow follow-through to extend only in the desired direction.

SKILLS PROGRESSIONS
FOR FOREHAND AND BACKHAND

Repetitions	Drills
5	1. From a ready position, obtain the correct grip. Release. Repeat.

The two-handed
backhand
pages 90-91.

Contact	Hit through	Follow-through high

Repetitions	Drills
10	2. From a ready position try the forward pivot, check foot position, recover.
10	3. Repeat #2 using the reverse pivot.
10	4. Using the forward pivot, take the complete backswing. Check the height of the racket head.
10	5. Using the forward pivot, combine the backswing, forward swing and the follow-through in one smooth motion.
25	6. From the back of the court, drop a ball in front of the desired side and stroke the ball into the fence 20 feet away. Recover to the ready position. Repeat.
30	7. Have a partner toss from the net (center) to the center line. Stroke using full pivot.
30	8. Toss from the net into the backcourt area (use a target) and stroke from the baseline into the opponent's court. Use full pivot.
15	9. Tosser will bounce and stroke a ball from the service line to partner at baseline on opposite side of the net. Pivot and stroke the ball back toward the tosser.
15	10. Hitter either drops ball or hits tossed ball into target area. (See diagram page 92 for accuracy drill.)

If a rebound wall is available

25	11. Drop a ball as in #6 and stroke it to a rebound wall. Catch the ball, drop and repeat.
20	12. Repeat #10, keep the ball to the right half of the forward rebound wall. Observe the net line.

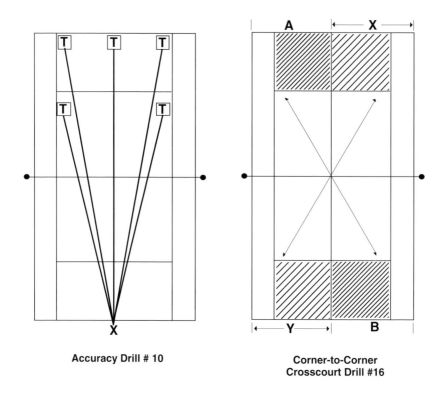

Accuracy Drill # 10

Corner-to-Corner
Crosscourt Drill #16

Repetitions	Drills
20	13. Repeat #11, keep the ball to the left half of the forward rebound wall. Observe the net line.
30	14. Try to replay the rebound against the forward wall. (Number of bounces is not important at this stage.)
30 min.	15. Drop a ball and stroke to your partner on the opposite side of the net. Try to continue as a rally.
30 min.	16. A and B, and X and Y keep the ball in play with a rally to the shaded areas shown on the court. Cover the area using forehand or backhand strokes only.

Name _____

Date _____ Section _____

Backhand Checklist

Using another player to rally with your partner, circle the appropriate letter as you observe your partner demonstrate his/her ability to use the backhand stroke. Allow appropriate warm-up time to determine accuracy in your observations.

Ratings: G = Good, F = Fair, P = Poor

G   F   P   1. Player uses the correct grip or a slight variation.

G   F   P   2. Anticipation is good, allowing sufficient time to move to the ball.

G   F   P   3. Proper footwork is used on the court.

G   F   P   4. Player steps into the ball with the right foot as contact is made.

G   F   P   5. Footwork is efficient—no wasted steps.

G   F   P   6. Backswing is taken back early and not rushed.

G   F   P   7. Topspin and/or slice is used effectively during the stroke.

G   F   P   8. Racket swing is relatively level into the incoming ball.

G   F   P   9. Contact with the ball is made in front of the right foot.

G   F   P   10. There is little or no wrist evident in the stroke.

G   F   P   11. The follow-through begins immediately as contact is made.

G   F   P   12. The follow-through flows smoothly to the completion of the stroke.

G   F   P   13. The racket head is high and in front of the right shoulder at the completion of the stroke.

G   F   P   14. Recovery is rapid, awaiting the next shot.

Comments: (use reverse side if needed)

Backhand Evaluation Comments:

Chapter 8: Evaluation

1. List at least five checkpoints in changing from the Eastern forehand grip to the Eastern backhand.

2. List as many tips for good backhand technique as you can.

3. Contrast the advantages and disadvantages of using the two-handed backhand. Which seems better? Why?

4. Explain the two choices of hand position for the two-handed backhand.

5. Why is footwork so important when using the two-handed backhand stroke?

6. Why does it seem advantageous for young player's to learn the two-handed backhand as compared to the single-handed?

7. Name at least two outstanding players who use the two-handed backhand.

8. Diagram five drills suited to the development of a strong backhand.

The Serve

Maurice McLaughlin set the tennis world on its ear in 1912 with a blistering serve that eventually won him the coveted U.S. Championship. Since that time, other tennis greats such as Pancho Gonzales, John McEnroe, Ivan Lendl, Boris Becker, Pete Sampras, Andre Agassi, Andy Roddick, and Roger Federer have decisively demonstrated that a tennis ball can be hit at speeds upward of 145 miles per hour and that the serve is the primary weapon of attack. Tennis authorities believe the serve to be the most important stroke of the game. There are three basic types of serves. Each is used for a specific reason, having its own strengths and weaknesses. An accomplished player will want to master all three. The three types are: (1) the slice serve, (2) the flat serve and (3) the twist or topspin serve.

THE SLICE SERVE

The slice serve is important to all tennis players. Since the ball has both sidespin and underspin, it is very difficult for an opponent to return this serve with excessive speed or precision. Hence, it is heavily relied upon as a second serve when the ball must be placed in play. To hit the serve, place the racket grip in a Continental position (halfway between forehand and back-hand). Your front foot should be at a 45° angle and approximately two to three feet from the center mark.

Stance

The initial stance for serving (in singles play) should be a position two to four feet from the center mark. This permits the server to bisect the angle of the return of serve, thus equalizing the distance required to move for the return. Feet and body should be in a throwing or hitting stance with the front toe at a 45° angle, about two inches behind the service line and on a line parallel to the intended path of the ball.

Stance

The slice serve

One necessary adjustment is to shift the toes so they are pointing at the right net post. Advanced players sometimes prefer to have both feet more parallel to the service line since this affords greater opportunity to uncoil the hips as the ball is being hit. If the ball is served too far to the left from this position, even after adjusting your aim and wrist movement, move the rear foot slightly back and to the rear of the front foot. This places the non-hitting shoulder more sideways to the net and should move the ball to the right.

The stance should be reasonably wide, at least shoulder-width, since this allows the server to shift weight to the back foot on the backswing and to the front foot during contact with the ball. As the toss is made, the rear foot should slide forward allowing a little more racket on impact with the ball.

At the moment of impact, the body should have a forward lean to reach the ball, but not with such momentum as to fall. The rear leg must be brought forward to support the body's weight. Remember to keep the front toe in contact with the ground throughout the toss and serve. This will insure that you do not foot fault and will provide a firm support base for hitting. As your service improves, you will likely extend your efforts to reach upward to the extent that you will thrust upward and leave the ground slightly. This is normal.

The Toss

Two balls should always be in possession of the server on the first serve of every point. The ball being hit should be pushed (not thrown) into the air to a height equal or slightly greater than can be reached with the racket arm fully extended. It cannot be stressed too highly that **serving faults are almost always caused by an inaccurate ball toss;** thus, it is important that you learn to toss the ball exactly where you wish it to go at all times. The toss

The slice serve, cont.

should be made so that the ball is thrown to a height of at least a fully-extended racket arm, and if allowed to drop, it should land about one foot to the right of your front toe and about one foot inside the court. This toss, which is slightly to the right of your body, will insure that sufficient slicing of the ball can occur. If the toss is not to the right, it will be nearly impossible to impart the sidespin, slicing action necessary to the serve.

The serve itself is generally broken down into three phases—the toss and backswing, the forward swing and the follow-through.

The backswing: The tossing arm and racket arm should begin the serve at least waist high with the ball hand touching the racket head. (See photos page 94.) As the left arm goes up, the racket arm drops down in a scissors or rocker motion, with the edge of the racket face leading. As the ball is released, the racket head begins an arc to a position behind the server's back with the elbow and wrist not yet cocked or bent. At this point the elbow and wrist begin to cock, allowing the racket head to move to a downward position almost touching the middle of the server's back.

The forward swing: As the ball descends the body weight shifts to the front foot, while the trunk and shoulders begin a forward rotation. As the wrist and elbow snap forward, the racket arm is fully extended **upward** at point of impact. The motion is often compared to throwing a ball or throwing a racket into the sky.

The follow-through: The follow-through is simply a continuation of the forward swing, making sure that the racket head ends up on the opposite side of your body and that the wrist fully uncocks so that it is pointing in the direction of the fence behind you and slightly downward. The right or back foot will cross the baseline to assist in maintaining body balance.

Common Slice Serve Errors

- Ball is not lifted as high as can be reached with the extended racket arm.
- Ball is not hit at the full extension point, but is allowed to drop a foot or more before hitting, causing elbow to bend.
- Ball is not thrown far enough to the right to allow the necessary slicing action.
- Wrist and elbow are not fully cocked. The checkpoint is "scratching the back."
- Incorrect grip is used, restricting the "slice" face on the racket.

THE FLAT SERVE

Most professionals rely upon the Continental grip to hit all serves, including flat, or no-spin serves. As the name implies, the ball is hit with the racket face square to the ball as opposed to attempting to cut off the right hand corner as in the slice serve. This gives the ball less spin, but more speed. The two serves might also be compared with throwing an overhand fast ball and a semi-sidearm curve. The key factor causing the racket face to meet the ball squarely is the angle of the wrist. If the wrist is bent straight back and brought straight through, then the ball will be hit with little or no spin. On the other hand, if you cock your wrist at an angle and snap through with a twist, as a curve ball pitcher does, then you will impart a slicing or spinning motion to the ball.

While the flat serve is very effective for reasonably tall—six feet or over—players, most short players will probably have more success with the slice serve. To hit the flat serve the ball must be tossed more off the left toe and not as far to the right as in the slice serve.

The Flat Serve

THE AMERICAN TWIST SERVE

The American twist or topspin is probably the most difficult serve to master, since it requires an unnatural arm motion. Its value lies in its use as a second serve, which has a high kicking action into the opponent's backhand. For doubles play, the high bounce allows the server more time to come in behind the serve, and when hit deep into the service court, keeps the receiver behind the baseline.

To execute the serve, hold the racket in an Eastern backhand grip. The ball must be tossed slightly behind the body and in back of the head. As the racket face moves to make contact, the server must hit up on the ball and at the same time snap the wrist hard over the top of the ball. Since the ball is tossed slightly behind the body, this will cause the server to bend backwards more, but will also cause an upward hitting motion. The impact point on the tennis ball should be at least 12 o'clock and with a topward rolling wrist motion. This motion resembles a brushing upward movement on the back of one's head. The follow-through is to the right side of the body.

PRACTICE HINTS FOR SERVING

1. Move in about halfway to the net and practice throwing a tennis ball into the proper service area. Throw vigorously using considerable wrist snap.
2. Now throw for the corners of the service area.
3. Gradually move to the baseline.
4. Practice the serving motion in front of a mirror. If the ceilings are too low use a table tennis paddle as a racket substitute.
5. Take a basket of balls and back off from the fence approximately 38 feet. Mark the fence either with an imaginary three-foot high line or attach several pieces of white tape in a line. Serve over the tape.
6. If having trouble serving from the baseline, move in about halfway—to the back of the service line. As speed and accuracy improve gradually back away until you are again behind the baseline.
7. Place racket covers or empty ball cans in critical serving areas and attempt to hit them with the serve.
8. Carry a basket or sack of old balls each time you go to the courts. Before leaving, always hit at least one sackful.
9. If you are having trouble synchronizing your toss and backswing, try tossing with the racket already cocked behind your back. Remember to take it all the way back to the "back scratching" position. This procedure is only a temporary measure and eventually it will be to your advantage to take a full windup.

The American Twist Serve

Serving Tips

- Take your time when serving. Plan the type of serve you wish to use and select the area of the receiving court into which you intend to hit the service. Don't rush! Bouncing the ball 3 to 4 times may help you to prepare.
- Position yourself properly at the baseline and don't change your basic position if using a different type of service. Otherwise, you may tip off the service you intend to use.
- Be consistent in your racket swing. This motion should be correct each time. The racket should not vary, since you maintain a firm grip on it.
- Raise the elbow to allow a smooth drop of the racket head behind the back.
- Practice enough to regulate your toss. The important aspects are ball position, height and direction. You cannot adjust the racket properly for a poor toss!
- Practice reaching upward to hit the ball. Hit with an upward stroke, rather than hitting the ball down into the opponent's court. Try hitting in the upward swing, just at the apex of the toss and swing—you'll find it works very well.
- Keep your service toss in front of your body to facilitate a forward motion into the net (attack) position.

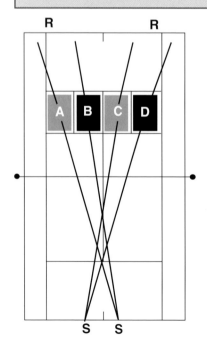

Service Target Areas

Learn to serve into the shaded areas of the court as shown. As you learn to do this you will (1) keep the ball deep in the service court and (2) serve to the opponent's forehand (A and C) or to the backhand (B and D).

QUESTIONS AND ANSWERS

How do I put more spin on my shots?
- Adjust grip to have a better angle on the face
- Use a thin gauge string with "string savers"
- String at a lower tension
- Use a larger head racket
- String with an open string pattern
- Brush across the ball more aggressively

What is the best defense against "spin artists?"
When you walk out on the court and see that your opponent is hitting with a Western grip you must decide to either keep the ball very high (with topspin) or very low (with underspin). Most topspinners have trouble with low short balls with underspin. If they are a two-hander, try keeping the ball short, low and in the corners of the service box.

How fast are the better players now hitting their service?
Modern technology has and still is rapidly changing the game. One of the more recent players at Wimbledon has been clocked with a 134 miles per hour serve. Also, several of the matches at Wimbledon recorded that more than half of all points ended before the third shot.

What would be the one best piece of advice for winning matches?
Arthur Ashe always said, "If you return the ball across the net five times on every point, you will rarely lose." In other words, keep the ball in play!

What are some checkpoints that might assist me in returning an opponent's serve?
Following is a brief review of service return:

Stance: slight crouch, square stance (like a baseball player) with weight on balls of feet and racket in forehand grip.

Position for return: depends on the server's position and the speed of the serve, i.e., you must bisect the angle of return. Thus, if the server moves farther from the center mark, you also must adjust to split your service court into two equal halves. Depth in or back from the service line depends on opponent's service speed.

Reading the ball toss: the farther the toss is away from the server the more slice. The closer the toss (12 o'clock) the more topspin and high kick.

The split step or hop: This loosens the weight of the body so that as the server makes contact you are moving slightly forward and are balanced to quickly move in either direction.

Learn to block the return: If service is hard, use the incoming speed to return the ball by "blocking" the ball, minimizing swing.

In a recent doubles match the receiver's partner was bouncing around and changing positions inside the service box just before my partner hit her serve. It was very distracting. Is this legal?
No. The receiver's partner cannot hinder the server in any way. The receiving team should automatically lose the point for "hindrance."

Where should I aim my serve?
If your serve is reliable enough to place the ball where you wish in the service court, then aim at the receiver's backhand. This is generally known as the weak side and hitting to this area will, by itself, often create errors in service returns.

Name _____

Date _____ Section_____

Service Checklist

Divide service courts in half—ten serves to each area. Circle the appropriate letter as you observe your partner demonstrate his/her ability to serve. Watch several serves to determine accuracy in recording your observations.

Ratings: G = Good, F = Fair, P = Poor

G F P   1. Footwork alignment is correct at the baseline.

G F P   2. Proper grip is used for the type of serve being attempted.

G F P   3. Release of ball on toss is at correct arm extension.

G F P   4. Height of toss is about 1 foot above racket reach.

G F P   5. Toss uses no wrist or elbow motion as lift is made.

G F P   6. Weight shifts properly into the stroke.

G F P   7. Elbow bends fully on racket backswing.

G F P   8. Ball is hit at full extension of arm.

G F P   9. Slight wrist action is used at contact.

G F P   10. Follow-through is across the body.

G F P   11. Service placement is satisfactory.

G F P   12. There is spin on the ball.

G F P   13. There is sufficient speed to keep the receiver deep.

Comments: (use reverse side if needed)

Service Evaluation Comments:

Chapter 9: Evaluation

1. List and describe the component parts of the slice serve.

2. What are the most common errors of the slice serve?

3. List the three basic serves and explain how each is different as to toss, stance, grip, contact and follow-through.

4. Which serve is most used as a second serve?

5. List five tips to improve your service.

6. What advice would you give to a student who is having trouble synchronizing ball toss and racket swing?

7. What are the advantages of keeping the service deep in the service area?

8. Describe the back scratch racket position used when serving the tennis ball.

Chapter 10
Auxiliary Strokes

In addition to the three basic strokes—forehand, backhand and service, there are several other types of returns that a player must make. These are the volley, the smash or overhead, the lob and the half-volley. As a player becomes proficient in the basic three, the opportunity presents itself to enlarge the depth of the strategy. This is done through the use of patterns of attack and defense developed through the execution of auxiliary strokes. A good player cannot be without them.

THE VOLLEY

The volley is the stroke used to return a ball before it comes into contact with the court. It is usually made from an opponent's drive. The shot is relatively simple, but it becomes more complicated as the tempo of the game increases.

A volley is usually made in the forecourt area—that is, closer to the net and well within the service court. It is an offensive stroke, often winning the point outright. Due to the close position to the net, angles can be used in the volley that frequently prohibit the opponent's return; thus, its effectiveness as an offensive weapon.

The Grip

Beginners and intermediates will find greater comfort using the Eastern forehand and backhand grips when hitting a volley. This grip has already been learned, is comfortable and adapts itself readily to the stroke. Eliminate all wrist action.

The forehand and backhand volleys

Basic Volley Positions

For high intermediates and advanced players, a service grip halfway between the Eastern forehand and backhand grip is preferred. This is primarily due to the increased tempo of the game, which prohibits a grip change while at the net. Experimentation and practice will determine which is best for the player according to the style and aggressiveness of that particular individual.

Ready for the Volley   **The Forehand Volley**

The Forehand Volley

High   **Medium**   **Low**

Forehand Volley Positions

High

Medium

Low

Basic Backhand Volley Positions

Backhand Volley Sequence

Footwork

The footwork patterns for the forehand and the backhand volleys are identical, just on opposite sides of the body. In most situations the player will use the basic forward pivot explained earlier. A slight bending of the knees is helpful as the execution is made.

Since the player is at the net position, the pace of the ball's approach may not allow time for exact footwork. In situations like this—and there are many of them—footwork is restricted and concentration on racket position is more important.

A "check stop" motion of the player will aid greatly in controlling the volley. Simply come to a brief pause just prior to making the intended shot. By pausing, a player is able to concentrate on the volley and move to the opponent's return. This may require a change of direction. The check stop or "split step" is used on the approach to the net.

The volley position can be a vulnerable one if the approach shots and volleys are not well executed. The opponent will attempt passing shots to either side that cause additional court coverage for the net player. In these situations, coverage is made as illustrated in the diagram.

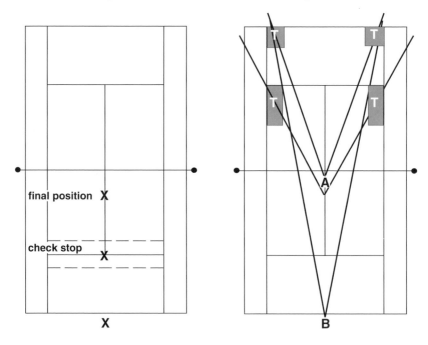

final position **X**

check stop **X**

X

Court positions for volley approach

B

Volley (A) may use a wide angle to mount the attack or use depth as a weapon. Compare this with the angle from baseline (B).

Cross-over step. This is a step and a pivot of the right foot and a large step across with the left foot, parallel to the net. This motion is accompanied by a rapid extension of the racket into the ball's path. The pattern allows almost all of the court to be covered using a comfortable, basic style of footwork. When used on the backhand side simply reverse the procedure.

Stroke Technique

The volley is not a stroke in the context of a forehand or a backhand. It is a stroke that blocks the incoming ball. As the ball approaches, hold the racket by the correct grip and move the face of the racket into the ball's path. A short backswing, about a foot in length, is recommended. Contact the ball with a short "punch." Aim the ball downward into the opponent's court, deep and at a sharp angle. A tight grip is mandatory to stabilize the stroke and to cope with the impact of the incoming ball.

When receiving balls that are above the net, try to punch through the ball at a downward angle. Be careful to clear the net sufficiently. On volleys made from below the height of the net, the player must exercise caution as the return flight of the ball must be angled upward. This may cause the ball to go out-of-bounds if the hitter is careless. As the ball approaches, the hitter bends the knees to "get down" with the ball. An effort should be made to keep the racket head and hand at the same level, parallel to the ground, on both the low backhand and forehand volley. As contact is made, a very firm grip is maintained, causing the blocking effect on the ball. There is very little follow-through and no swinging action.

Court Position

Singles: As the player receives the opportunity to go to the net, he returns the short ball away from the opponent. This is usually to an open part of the court and at an angle away from the other player. The direction of the approach shot will determine the position of the net player. The approach shot should have good pace and be deep to the open area of the court. If the receiver is in the home position, place the approach shot deep to the backhand corner, as this is frequently the weakest side, and many players are unable to handle the pressure created by the approaching net rusher.

When receiving a short ball as you go to the net, caution must be used when executing the approach shot, because (1) the ball will frequently be below the height of the net and (2) the distance between the point of contact and the opponent's baseline has shortened. Thus, when the total body weight is moved forward in a running pattern it is extremely easy to over hit the ball, causing the shot to go out of bounds.

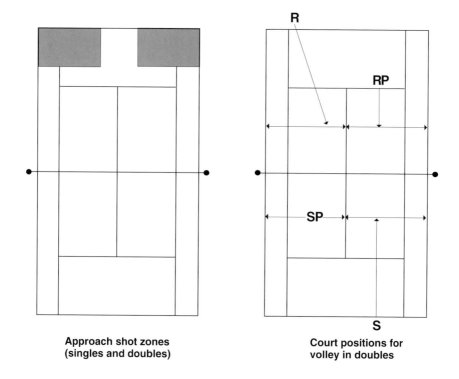

**Approach shot zones
(singles and doubles)**

**Court positions for
volley in doubles**

As the approach shot is made, the hitter is positioned about eight feet from the net on the side in which the ball is hit, but close to the midcourt line. This position allows maximum court coverage. For approach shots that may go down the middle, the only position to obtain is one in the center of the forecourt area.

Doubles: The volley position in doubles is slightly different because two players cover the court. Each player, being responsible for one side, should be in position halfway between the doubles sideline and the midcourt line. Ideally, both players assume the net position together—the server/receiver joining his or her partner at the net. Coverage of all shots should be complete if both players work harmoniously. Shots going down the center are usually taken by the player with the forehand return.

Each point should be played aggressively so it can be won quickly, rather than simply keeping the ball in play. Make crisp, sharp shots. In doubles, aim at an angle that will win the point outright, down the center between opponents, or aim your volley at the feet of the closest net player.

Common Volley Errors

Volley goes out of bounds. Tighten grip and restrict the amount of backswing used to punch the ball. Also, limit the amount of follow-through to increase the length of your ball. Hit in front of your body.

Volley has no speed or crispness. Prepare earlier to meet the ball in front of the body for both backhand and forehand. Anticipate well, step into the shot. Watch the ball closely, contacting the ball in the center of the racket face. Punch the ball with a slight downward chop, keep the wrist firm.

Defensive body volleys lacking pace. Use backhand volley and grip. Move feet into the ball as it approaches. Contact the ball well out in front. Anticipate early.

THE OVERHEAD SMASH

When playing the net in the forecourt position and your opponent hits a short high ball easily within reach, prepare to hit the smash, or overhead, as it is commonly called. The overhead is the most spectacular shot of tennis and is frequently used to win the point outright. Although the shot can be hit from any position on the court, the chances for error become much greater as the player approaches the backcourt area. The closer to the net the better, as the angles are greater and the height of the bounce can be effective—sometimes going over the reach of the opponent's racket.

The Overhead Smash Sequence

For the initial movement, turn sideways to the net and to the incoming ball. Using the basic side-step motion, move back under the ball, keeping the ball in front of the body at all times. At a point where you anticipate the ball will land, place the weight on both feet, favoring the rear foot primarily. As the stroke is made, shift the weight forward into the stroke, straightening the knees as the reach is extended into the ball. Concentrate on keeping the feet at a 45° angle to the net and to the ball as you shift the body forward. This is comfortable because it closely resembles the serving position.

The Grip

The Eastern forehand grip is the basic grip for the overhead due to the familiarity already established with the forehand. Other grips may be used, including a service grip, a grip halfway between the forehand and the backhand, and/or an Eastern backhand grip. The latter is used primarily by advanced players. The timing is more critical, however, and the grip causes a closed face on the racket, pulling the ball sharply down into the opponent's court. Grip style depends largely on the players skill. A more skillful player will use either the slice grip or the backhand.

Footwork

As with any stroke in tennis, footwork becomes one of the most important ingredients. Proper footwork moves the player into position to play the ball correctly. When hitting the overhead, footwork begins as soon as the high arc of the incoming ball is recognized. Anticipate where the ball is going and move your body to this particular area.

The scissors kick overhead is a method of reaching a ball that is a step away (behind the body). The scissor kick is a balance maneuver to allow immediate recovery combined with a powerful stroke. A side view is shown above.

Stroke Technique

Basic preparation for the overhead, as with most tennis strokes, consists of the backswing, the contact point and the follow-through.

Since the original position is at the net, assume that a ready position is maintained. First, change the grip. Turn sideways to the net, taking the racket back into the drop-back position behind the back. With the other arm, point toward the incoming ball. This motion is excellent for balance. Continue the racket in the backswing position, elbow high, racket head dipping well behind the back. As the ball approaches the contact point, swing the racket head upward into the ball. Contact the ball slightly out in front of the body at about one o'clock. Bring the wrist into the ball very slightly to get the angle down onto the court. Try to hit **up** and over the ball rather than down onto the ball. The follow-through is to the opposite side of the body. Recovery should be quick, as many overheads are returned.

Overhead Court Position

The court position is usually in the forecourt area. Most overheads are hit from the service courts, although the stroke may be hit from any part of the court. For consistency, accuracy, and better placement, use the forecourt area. Allow the ball to bounce before using the overhead to hit very high incoming balls. This will provide for better timing in the execution.

Use of the overhead in both singles and doubles depends entirely on the effectiveness of the offensive and defensive strokes. Strategy also plays a very important part in maneuvering the opponent into positions where the lob will be used, as it is this stroke that causes the overhead to come into play.

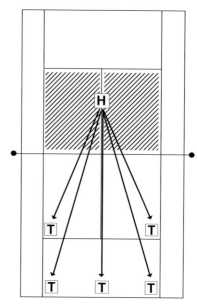

Overhead target areas: Use angles and/or depth

How to play the overhead smash

Hitting Zones: Play it Safe

Zone A:
Careful here—half speed smash. Keep opponent deep with your return. Let it bounce.

Zone B:
Use a three-fourths smash, keeping pressure on the opponent; maintain your position and move to the net.

Zone C:
Go for the winner—everything is in your favor at this position at the net.

Overhead Smash Tips

- Watch the ball at all times and "point the ball in" with the opposite hand.
- Take the racket back early, behind the back.
- Don't "get set" too early; keep moving the feet.
- Stroke smoothly and aggressively.
- Lead with the racket head; use the proper grip.
- Contact the ball with the arm at a full extension.
- Follow through with the racket to the left side (diagonally across).
- Recover quickly in case of a return by your opponent.
- Practice frequently, using more power as control is established.

Common Overhead Errors

Ball goes long. The ball is hit early and the racket is making contact before the ball passes "one o'clock." The racket face is open at contact. Concentrate on hitting with the proper grip to bring the tennis ball down. Do not lead with your wrist.

Ball goes into the net. Stroke **upward** more strongly. Drop the racket head behind the back before the upward swing. Don't let it drop too low.

No power into the ball. Bend the elbow totally, and throw the racket upward into the ball. Use the wrist more effectively.

THE LOB

If you can picture in your mind the arc of a rainbow, you can visualize the trajectory of the lob. This is probably one of the least used and practiced strokes in tennis. It is not a complicated shot, but most players would rather use another stroke when trying to get away from a difficult problem—such as being pressed deep into a corner.

The lob can be either offensive or defensive. However, it is used primarily as a defensive shot. It is rarely practiced to the degree that the technique is mastered. The well-executed lob can be troublesome to an opponent. The main objectives in lobbing are (1) to give yourself more time to recover, (2) to push the opponent(s) away from the net and (3) to change pace in your game plan.

The Grip

Use either the Eastern forehand or backhand grip. The lob is actually either a forehand or a backhand ground stroke, so the grip will follow the respective shot.

Footwork

As with any ground stroke, proper footwork helps with successful execution. Earlier discussions on proper patterns of footwork should be followed. When the player is "set" in the correct position, there is a much stronger chance that the shot will be hit firmly, achieve the proper height and obtain sufficient depth to be effective.

Stroking Technique

Getting into position is of utmost importance. When the incoming ball approaches, move into position as early as possible. Have the racket back by the time the ball bounces. From the backswing position, with knees bent, bring the racket slightly under the ball as the forward swing begins. Lift and height will be achieved by hitting upward on the shot.

When approaching the contact point with the ball, begin the lift rapidly as though the follow-through is starting. This will create a high arch on the shot, sufficient to clear the forecourt position occupied by the opponent. If desired, dropping the racket head earlier will allow for more height. This may, however, telegraph the shot to your opponent.

The follow-through is most important, as it will serve to guide the ball in the intended direction and height. The follow-through also puts spin on the ball.

It should be noted that the normal stroking technique remains the same as a regular forehand or backhand—comfort in the grip and an arm stroke, using the entire arm and racket as one moving extension to stroke the ball. Restrict the use of the wrist as much as possible.

Offensive versus Defensive Lobs

Both offensive and defensive lobs are very effective when used properly. The primary differences are found in the direction, disguise, height and spin of the ball. The offensive lob is used as a weapon against an unsuspecting opponent. The stroke can be an outright point winner.

The defensive lob, on the other hand, is usually anticipated by the opponent, because the player receiving the ball is obviously pressed and needs time to recover. The pressed player hits a defensive lob up into the air and deep into the backcourt.

By definition, an **offensive lob** is a well disguised lob with a normal forehand or backhand swing. However, as the racket meets the ball, a lift is

Target Area for Lobs
(H=Hitter) (F=Feeder)

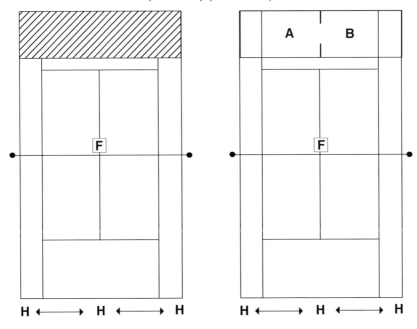

Zone A: Best (forehand side)
Zone B: Best (backhand side)

provided that creates moderate topspin. The trajectory causes the ball to go over the outstretched reach of the opponent.

When the ball hits the ground, the topspin causes the ball to jump away from the net, making it a difficult shot to return. If executed well and used discreetly, it is very effective. If the shot is not hit well, it will probably fall short, well within the reach of the opponent.

The **defensive lob** is a much less disguised stroke. The attacking player knows that the defensive lob is a frequently used shot to nullify an effective net approach. The defensive lob is easier to return than the offensive lob due to the height of the lob. The defensive lob should land deep in the backcourt area, close to the baseline.

When attempting either lob, aim the shot toward the opponent's **backhand corner**. This is the weakest area of return, and if the stroke is short, the opponent will have trouble putting the ball away on the high backhand shot. Many times, when the opponent can reach the ball, he or she carefully drives it over using an uncomfortable high volley. This can easily be set up for the alert lobber. However, if the lob is to the forehand, a return is somewhat easier to achieve and—if the shot is low and within reach—watch out for the overhead that is sure to come. Remember, practice makes a big difference.

Common Lob Errors

Lobs are too short. Secure your position earlier. Use the arm more in making the stroke. Drive up and through the ball. Follow-through fully. "Carry" the ball on the strings as long as possible.

Ball is often mis-hit. Get ready early. Watch the ball more closely. See the ball into the strings of the racket. Don't change your mind during the stoke. If you're going to lob, do it!

Offensive lobs are frequently "put away." Don't "go to the well" too often. Be discreet, use lobs sparingly, preferably from inside the baseline. The deeper you are when you use the lob, the more time the opponent has to reach the ball due to the low trajectory. Topspin lobs are very difficult to execute. Don't use them very much.

Lob Technique Tips

- Get into position quickly.
- Use proper footwork.
- Disguise your intentions if possible.
- Stroke firmly upward into the ball, using a full follow-through.
- Keep the racket "on the ball" as long as possible.
- Recover quickly for the return.

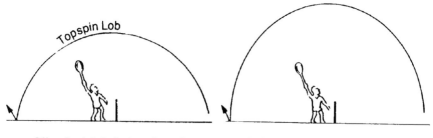

Offensive lob trajectory (lower)
(rarely used)

Defensive lob trajectory (higher)
(frequently used)

HALF-VOLLEY

The half-volley is primarily a defensive shot that is neither a volley nor a full ground stroke. It is used when a player is caught in a court position with the ball bouncing at the feet, which is usually on either an advance to a net position and in "no man's land." Another word for the half-volley is the "trap shot," since a player simply places the racket behind the anticipated point of bounce and allows the ball to deflect from the racket face. The stroke is adjusted by keeping both backswing and follow-through to a minimum. Most of the power for the shot is provided by the ball's rebound speed. The point of impact should be slightly in front of your body.

An analogy that might be used for this shot is the play of a baseball infielder. Often, infielders will have to "stab with their gloves" at a point where they think the ball will rebound from the playing field. The difference between baseball and tennis is that the tennis player uses a racket rather than a glove.

The grip for the half-volley is the same as for the forehand and backhand. Remember to use a check stop approach as is required in the volley, keeping the knees bent and the head of the racket nearly parallel to the ground. Also, a short backswing followed by a short follow-through is necessary as you continue to the net position.

The angle of the racket face determines the ball's angle of deflection. Of course, the closer to the net the more open the face of the racket needs to be to raise the ball. A backcourt half-volley will require the face of the racket to be more closed to prevent the ball from rising too high. Have patience. Most beginners find that mastering this shot requires considerable practice.

Half-Volley, approaching the bounce

THE DROP SHOT

More points have been lost by hitting drop shots than have been won. It is not a high percentage shot. However, there are times in every match when the right shot may be that soft and delicate forehand or backhand slice that barely trickles over the net and dies on impact. It can be a physically and psychologically devastating weapon when used in an effective manner. Some of the more general principles that govern the drop shot are:

- Drop shots into the wind are more effective than with the wind.

- Drop shots in doubles are usually a no-no.

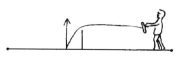

Drop shot trajectory—
heavy backspin

- The harder the surface, the fewer the drop shots.

- The best offense against a drop shot is a return drop shot.

- Drop shots have backspin; move into the ball because the ball will not come to you.

Drop shot trajectory—
light backspin

- Do not drop shot from the baseline. Drop only on short balls and then usually at a point across the net that is closest to you.

- Most drop shots are hit with a chopping or slice motion. Always watch the head of your opponent's racket. When the head of the racket is raised higher than the handle, the shot must be a chop shot or drop shot. Move forward since the backspin will prevent the ball from bouncing to you.

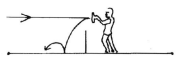

Drop shot trajectory—
drop volley at net

Chapter 10: Evaluation

1. What are three of the most common errors associated with the volley?

2. List at least five tips in technique to improve your volley.

3. If a player is consistently hitting long on the overhead stroke, what advice would you give?

4. Give at least three reasons for using a lob.

5. Contrast a defensive lob and an offensive lob.

6. What are some of the more common errors associated with the lob?

7. Describe the check stop and how it is used to prepare for the volley.

8. What is the half-volley and when is it used?

9. List six principles to keep in mind when hitting a drop shot.

Singles Strategy

THE PERCENTAGE THEORY

"If I can somehow manage to hit one more ball back than you, I'll win this point." This is the philosophy of the tennis player who attempts to pursue the percentage theory. Keeping the ball in play should be paramount in the mind of every player. Understandably, this is sometimes very hard to do.

It is well-known that most tennis matches are won on errors. Average and above-average players sometimes defeat themselves by making too many mistakes. These players hit one or two balls back, then get impatient and try to force an opening without the proper tools. Thus, they make an error, giving the opponent another point.

In good tennis circles, the player who makes the fewest errors or mistakes usually wins. In a match between players A and B, a close analysis would show that if A is the winner, close to 80 percent of the points won by A are due to common errors made by B. The 20 percent of the points A won by forcing shots, placements or aces, are not sufficient to cause B much of a problem. These percentages show that careless mistakes must be reduced. Careless mistakes can occur throughout the entire range of tennis skills and can include not watching the ball, improper footwork, poor stroke technique and lack of strategy. To be a "pusher," as the retriever is called, is a true compliment.

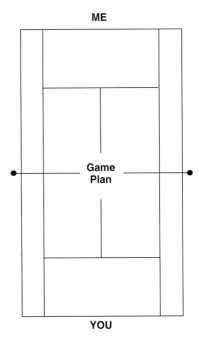

Players on the opposite side of the net from a pusher are in for a long day. They will either have to play the same game as the pusher—a task they have neither the skill nor the patience to achieve— or they must attack and defeat the pusher using placement, power and a forcing type game. Not many players have this expertise either. After several hours of play, pushers usually emerge the winners.

To play percentage tennis, a person must develop an optimum level of conditioning, for this requires a tremendous amount of running to keep the ball in play. A full knowledge of techniques is necessary, as correct execution will be demanded in the strokes. A sound knowledge of strategy is also expected, since the retriever needs to understand the opponent's intent and be able to counter this with early anticipation, preparation and proper stroke selection.

This is not an easy undertaking. It requires all the qualities mentioned previously, plus great determination. The primary ingredients of percentage tennis are patience and conditioning. Without patience, the percentage theory is not a realistic goal.

THE DEPTH THEORY

Simply stated, this theory involves the consistent practice of stroking the ball deep into the opponent's backcourt. It is an effective way to keep an opponent from mounting an attack. Imagine being in home position with two feet behind the baseline. An opponent strokes a deep ball that lands just inside the line. You have two choices: (1) back up, giving ground, and play the return from six to eight feet deep; or (2) play the ball from the present position using a half-volley. Your choice will be mandated by your skill level and perhaps the pace of the incoming ball.

An aggressive player wants to attack the opponent at the earliest opportunity, knowing that this additional pressure by *itself* frequently creates a stroking error. The attacker waits for a short ball, moves in, hits an effective approach shot and secures the net position. By keeping the ball deep, a player accomplishes the following:

- Keeps the opponent away from the net (attack) position.
- Allows more time to prepare for each stroke, since the incoming ball is hit from the opponent's backcourt.
- Provides added opportunities to attack, since the opponent's depth in the backcourt causes many short returns to be hit.
- Secures court position, since the possible angles of return become smaller due to the depth of the hitter.
- Prevents the opponent from scoring an ace, because the opponent cannot establish the critical angle or speed desired. The shot is hit from too far away and must travel too far in the air before reaching the other side of the net. The length of the shot provides you with the time needed to make another successful return.

The depth theory is especially pertinent in volleying. Hit the ball away from your opponent and deep to the backcourt area, allowing little or no time for a return shot. Short angles are excellent, provided they win the point outright. However, short angles and careless volleys that land in the middle of the opponent's court create havoc for any net player and frequently cause the loss of the point. It is an uncomfortable feeling, after establishing a position at the net, to volley short and bring the opponent to the attack zone. You feel like a target and are rightly intimidated. Keep the volley deep and stay out of trouble.

Court Position

Most players return to the home position, one to three feet behind the center mark, after hitting the ball. A proficient player's success will be due, in part, to the ability to observe an opponent and anticipate the next move. That is, you may suspect that your opponent will stroke the ball to the open court area rather than directly back to you, because this is also your strategy. Careful observation of your opponent's footwork and body position will tell you the intended direction of the stroke. However, you cannot be 100 percent positive, so you must anticipated all possibilities.

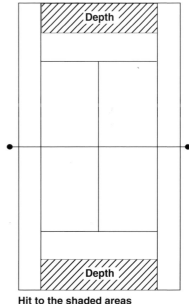

Hit to the shaded areas

Bisecting the angles of return. When you bisect the angle of return, you are splitting the distance between where the ball can be hit—to your right and left—with you in the center of that angle. This is true on service, ground strokes and volleys. When properly positioned, a player will have equal distance to cover on forehand and backhand.

Observe where your opponent stands when receiving service and during play. Frequently an opponent will be standing much to the left of the center of the angle described above. This will probably indicate a weak backhand and an attempt to cover for it.

No man's land. Generally, tennis play occurs in either the backcourt area or at the net. Beginners and intermediates will stay in the backcourt while advanced players will develop the serve and volley game. The normal drive coming over the net usually lands within a yard of the service line, in the area

No man's land

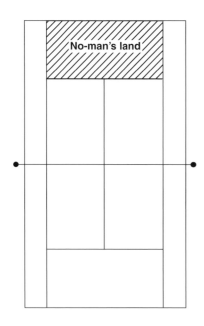

commonly referred to as no man's land. This area is between the baseline (backcourt) area and the volley (forecourt) position. Young or inexperienced players frequently play in this area, making it their home position. Problems occur when incoming balls land at a player's feet or go by as much as head high. Playing in this position creates anxiety when trying to return the low shots successfully and when trying to determine if those balls going past—still in the air—are going to go out of bounds or land inside the court. Luck seems to say that those high ones you hit would have gone out, and those you let go always drop inside the baseline. If you play in no man's land, pointwise "you get killed." Since this position is not close enough to the net to volley the ball effectively, nor deep enough to allow sufficient time to position yourself properly, you can easily be the recipient of sharp crosscourt strokes or drives that go down the line.

Frequently you must move into no man's land to play a short ball. Once you play it, however, continue on into the net or return to your baseline. **Do not remain in the center of the court.**

SERVICE STRATEGY

Choosing the Right Serve

As mentioned earlier, there are three basic serves: the flat serve, the slice serve and the twist or topspin. Every advanced player should develop the ability to execute each serve properly. One type of service is often more effective than another against an opponent. Discovering which type of serve gives your opponent the most trouble and using this serve to maximum benefit is an important skill.

On the right side of the baseline, the server usually stands between one and three feet from the center mark. This remains the same no matter which serve is used. The angle of this position promotes service to the opponent's backhand and allows for proper court coverage on service returns. It is permissible to stand as far to the right as the singles sideline, although this is rarely done due to the amount of court area left open on the backhand side.

When serving from the left side of the baseline, the server's position is about three to five feet from the center mark. Most players stand a little farther away from the center mark on this side due to: (1) a desire to get a sharper angle toward the opponent's backhand and (2) a feeling of more security toward the forehand side for returned serves.

Right service court

Left service court

The keynote to serving is variety. There is a significant advantage in hitting different types of serves to your opponent. Determine early in a match which serve seems to give your opponent the most difficulty and use this serve most of the time. Hit about 85 percent of your serves to the receiver's *backhand*, as this usually creates many errors in service returns. Many returns from poor backhands will be so weak that they can easily be attacked.

Vary the type of service used. If your favorite serve is a slice service to the backhand, occasionally use a topspin or flat serve to change the pace. This often creates an error by throwing the opponent off insofar as timing and positioning are concerned. Move your opponent around as you serve. Place most serves to the backhand, some to the forehand and some directly into the body. The slice service toward the backhand that curves into the body is extremely effective when used discretely.

Frequently the first and second serves vary greatly. Many inexperienced players serve a very hard, inaccurate ball on the first effort, then follow with a

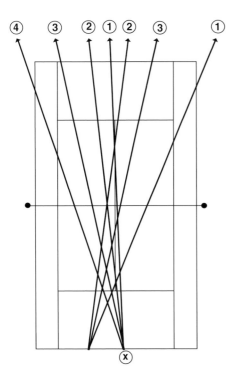

Placement of service, forehand and backhand courts in order of preference.

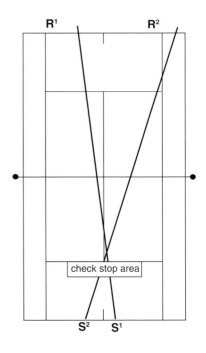

Service Approach Check: Server should pause at the check stop area when following serve to the net, read the service return, then continue.

very slow-paced ball that, while secure from a double fault, does nothing other than put the point in play. This second serve can easily be handled by the receiver, who usually puts the server on the defensive by hitting a solid, well-placed return.

A better procedure is to serve two balls of about the same speed but with different types of spin; for example, a flat first serve followed by a slice or a topspin. Another combination is to use a slice service as a first serve, followed by a twist (topspin). The use of spin—either slice or topspin—gives more clearance to the ball as it goes over the net. As a result, it is more secure against the double fault.

Remember these basic points:

1. **Placement:** First get the ball into the service court. If possible, go deep to the opponent's backhand, directly at the opponent or to the forehand corner.
2. **Speed:** Serve with sufficient speed to keep the opponent in the backcourt area when returning the serve. Increase speed only when you can maintain control.
3. **Spin:** Use enough spin to allow the ball to clear the net, then to take the ball down on the court, and enough spin to curve the ball in the desired direction (slice) or to kick up a higher bounce on contact with the court (twist).
4. **Variety:** Keep your opponent guessing. If you serve to the same spot again and again, your opponent will adjust and begin returning more effectively. Mix them up!

If serve and volley tactics are your basic strategy, decide whether a speed or a spin serve is most effective against your opponent. If your opponent handles speed well, the ball may be returned before you can establish your position for the approach volley. Thus, a slow spin serve might be more advantageous. On the other hand, if your favorite serve is a spin serve, but due to the slower speed your opponent handles it easily and causes you to make errors, you have another problem. There are things you must "feel" out as you begin playing the match. Think the problem through. Then do whatever is best in the given situation.

If you are primarily a baseline player—i.e., you stay in the backcourt area—you are part of the large majority of tennis players. The baseline player uses the service as a means of starting the point. On occasion, a hard hit serve will win the point by itself. However, a player will often use ground strokes to win the point, coming to the net only as a matter of necessity when a very short ball is received. Beginning and intermediate tennis is played with this strategy in mind.

STRATEGY WHEN RECEIVING SERVICE

As your opponent prepares to serve, you will probably have many things going through your mind. "Where should I stand?" "What type of serve will be used?" "Will the server come to the net? "How fast will the serve be hit?"

Many leading tennis professionals agree that the **service** is the most important stroke in tennis. If this is true, then the **service return** must be equally as important from the receiver's point of view. If you can win the games you serve and break the opponent's serve one time, you will win the set. Being able to return the serve effectively is extremely important. Here are the key points in returning service:

1. *Place the ball in play.* Try not to make an error on the return. This is the most important factor in receiving service. Give the opponent a chance to make an error. **Return the ball.**
2. Maintain a court position according to the opponent's serve. Remember to bisect the angle of return, allowing equal coverage to the forehand and the backhand.

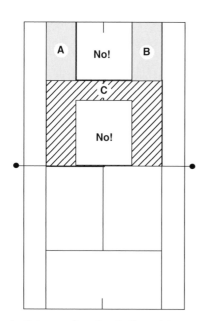

1. **Return to A or B only if receiving on that side. Don't return deep crosscourt against a net rusher.**
2. **Return to C should be good anytime, but keep the return *low*.**

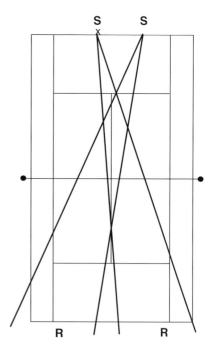

Bisecting angles of return (service)

3. If the opponent stays at the baseline, try for a medium speed return to the backcourt. If you do this effectively, the service advantage is lost. Concentrate on playing out the point. If you get a short return, drive deep to the backhand corner and then take the net position.

4. If the opponent uses a serve and volley strategy follow these points:

   a. *Stay calm,* concentrate, anticipate the serve.

   b. *Keep the return low*—usually to the feet at the service line as the server comes toward the net. If possible, move in on the service to cut down on the time the server has to get to the net.

   c. If the service is hard, with spin, just try to *block it* back with a slight chip using backspin. Disregard using a full ground stroke technique. Try for a low return.

   d. Aim the ball down the sideline. This causes the server to change direction on the approach. However, if you go to the center of the court due to lack of time for preparation, this is satisfactory. Also, the net is lowest at this point.

   e. Attack the opponent's approach shot. If you hit a good service return, you can capitalize on your next shot. Use lobs and drives effectively now.

   f. Occasionally use the lob to throw the opponent off guard. Lob toward the backhand side.

   g. Be consistent; avoid careless errors. Give your opponents the opportunity to beat themselves. Patience is required.

TYPES OF GAMES

A player's skill determines the style of play that may be used effectively. Skill levels are determined primarily by the competency established in practice patterns using the strokes of the game.

1. **3-Stroke Game:** uses the service, forehand and backhand only. This is played as a baseline game, whether singles or doubles.

2. **5-Stroke Game:** uses the three strokes mentioned above plus the volley and the smash. This is a more aggressive style of play frequently found in intermediate tennis.

3. **All-Court Game:** uses all of the strokes mentioned above plus the auxiliary shots including the offensive and defensive lob, half-volley, chop and drop shots, lob volley and the drop volley. There are not many intermediate players who have command of all these strokes, and probably very few advanced players. This skill level is primarily found in higher levels of competitive play. Even then, many of these shots are not used effectively.

No matter what your style of play, there is always room for improvement.

Basic Points of Singles Strategy

1. Keep the ball in play. Give your opponent another chance to make an error. Most games are won because of an opponent's mistakes.

2. When possible, keep the play to the opponent's backhand, as this is usually the weaker of the two ground strokes.

3. Look for openings in your service attack—*move* the receiver. If, as you toss the ball, the receiver moves to cover your service to the backhand with a forehand return, then occasionally direct your serve to the forehand corner. Aim the serve at the receiver's body once in a while for variety.

4. Mount an attack on any short ball you receive. By coming to the net and driving deep to the opponent's backhand on the approach, you force the opponent to (1) worry about your attack, (2) hit a winner, (3) force an error on your part, (4) lob (most likely up to the advanced level).

5. Success in establishing control of the net is based on your approach shot, its accuracy and depth.

6. Occasional play to your opponent's forehand opens up opportunities for attacking the backhand area. Keep your opponent deep.

7. Use the strokes that give you the highest percentage of success given the situation at hand.

8. Be careful about using drop shots and drop volleys. They have a low percentage of success and often cause much trouble to the hitter.

9. Use a check stop on your way to the net as it greatly facilitates movement laterally to play the incoming ball.

10. When playing against a net rusher, use the stroke that you have the most confidence in and the one that has the greatest percentage for success.

11. Place your return at the feet of the net rusher, causing an upward volley on the ball to clear the net. A short return may allow you the chance to move in for the kill.

QUESTIONS AND ANSWERS ABOUT PLAYING

After hitting a very good lob I tend to watch from behind my baseline. Is this bad?
It's not good. By hitting a great lob over your opponent at the net, you put your opponent in a defensive position. You should move to the net, forcing the opponent into a lower percentage shot.

I follow my serve to the net but do not seem to be getting in far enough for my first check stop and volley.
First, you could just be slow. Second, you might be throwing your toss either too far behind you (for topspin) or too far to the right so that your first step is not straight in toward the net. Be sure to move forward with the follow-through. Don't wait to see if the serve is good before you go.

How can I avoid being caught by a quick lob over my head?
You may be closing too tightly on the net. Know who the good lobbers are and when you see a lob situation and/or motion, back pedal a few steps for protection. It is always easier to close back in if an opponent hits a short shot, than to retreat.

What can I do when an opponent destroys me with a serve and volley game?
It could be the opponent is just a better player; however, you might try the following:
1. Determine whether you are losing the points by missing the return of serve or whether your opponent is winning the points with the volley. If you are missing the service return, make up your mind ahead of time where you are going to return the ball. If the serve is on your backhand, go down the line; if it is on your forehand, go crosscourt. The important thing is to put the ball in play.
2. If you have been chipping the ball at your opponent's feet and your opponent is still putting the volley away, try hitting out a little more.
3. Run around a weak second serve for a forehand.
4. Moving back will give you more time, but this allows your opponent to close more tightly. Moving in tight against the less powerful serve often forces mistakes.
5. Make your opponent change the volley pattern. If your opponent is going cross-court for safe volleys, then move early in that direction, forcing a change of shot.
6. Use the lob to throw the opponent off stride. Lob to the backhand.

What one or two tips would help someone who can only play once or twice a week?

Most pros agree that getting the racket back early and physical conditioning are probably the two most important tips for a weekend player.

What do you think of the practice of wearing rings and watches while playing? Some pros do.

The pros generally wear these objects because they are endorsements and they are being paid to do so. Anything that is distracting or interferes with your "touch" or "feel" of the racket will hamper your performance.

Why is my first serve erratic and seldom in, but my second serve very reliable?

You probably hit the first serve too hard. Check the fundamentals—take your time, concentrate and slow the serve down. Keep the toss in front of your body and high enough to really reach for it. It will work; give it time and lots of practice. Also, back away from using so much speed, but use more spin. Develop two medium-paced serves rather than a hard first serve and a soft second serve.

Every time I hit a return back that lands short, my opponent comes to the net. This really bothers me. What can I do to eliminate this problem?

Raise your stroke trajectory and hit the ball deeper into your opponent's court. You give your opponent the opportunity to come to the net when you hit short. Lengthen your backswing and follow-through to acquire more depth.

What can I do to win more points? I seem to beat myself.

Understand the meaning of percentage tennis; realize the importance of getting *each and every* ball back over the net. Anticipate early, set up quickly and aim for the backcourt area. Review basic fundamentals. Give yourself good net clearance. Practice this procedure frequently. You should improve dramatically!

I am usually late in my swing trying to return my opponent's hard serve. What can I do to improve my return percentage?

Your problem is a lack of time to accomplish a full swing in your return. Try blocking the ball back with a little underspin. You should see good results quickly.

How can I know whether my opponent is going to hit flat, topspin, or slice service?

Most tennis players do not study their opponents enough. Your first clue will be the toss and the grip the opponent uses. A toss out to the side probably indicates a slice; a toss to the left and behind the head means topspin; and a toss straight up usually means a hard and flat serve. Remember also that the more your opponent shifts his or her hand from an Eastern grip to the backhand, the more spin you will be looking at. Returning a very fast serve requires a fast turn-hit motion. This means the racket must be cocked as you turn so the result is a step-hit motion much like a one-two punch. One way to speed up the process is to first determine the direction of the ball by the toss, then take a very slight hop in that direction to get your weight flowing forward and on the balls of your feet. From there on it depends on your skill level.

What advice do you have for playing against two-handers?

There are several things you might try doing.

- Hit straight at a two-hander. This prevents the free-swinging two-hander from getting that big, looping swing.
- Try short shots into the midcourt area. Two-handers usually prefer a baseline game and either must do a lot of running up and back or play in less familiar territory.
- Hit low slicing shots. The low bouncing shot prevents the two-hander from effectively stiffening the left hand to generate power.
- Aim for the T-zone—where the singles sidelines meet the service line. Low wide shots are tough for two-handers.
- Don't worry about too many different kinds of shots from two-handers— only topspin and lots of it.

As a serve and volley player, what can I do for an edge against the hard-hitting two hander?

1. Since most two-handers hit topspin returns and topspin players prefer to hit higher balls, slice the serve a lot and keep it low.
2. Most two-handers like to "groove" on a serve so it is critical that you never give away location or type of serve. In short, you must keep them guessing.
3. Since the two-hander likes to hit at the high point of the bounce, this affords you more time to close in on the net. It is important that you close as tightly as possible, but use the check stop to read the incoming shot.

What is the one best piece of advice for a beginning tennis player? Set realistic goals according to your aspirations. This means that if you want to be a tournament player, your training program will be at a different level than if your goal is to be a good club player who plays for self-enjoyment and exercise.

What one tip could you give me to play better on clay?

It has been said that clay and other soft surfaces favor the thinking player. Be prepared to play long points by maintaining concentration and setting up your shots in a series.

What advice do you have for winning a tiebreaker?
Every point is a key point. In a regular game you can get fancy once in a while or go for the big one, and if it doesn't work, you can still retrench and possibly win. The tiebreaker does not allow much room to recover once you fall behind. Play the tiebreaker exactly as you played to get there. Remember to hit your high percentage shots and, above all, "hang in there." You will be amazed at how many of your opponents will fold if you are patient and persistent.

As a recreational or club player, why should I learn to hit topspin?
The main reason is control plus speed. Topspin allows you to hit the ball harder, because the spin on the ball causes it to drop rapidly after crossing the net.

Chapter 11: Evaluation

1. Describe the court area known as no man's land.

2. What do you do when you bisect the angle of return?

3. Locate the basic home position on a tennis court.

4. What is the best thing to do to prevent your opponent from repeatedly taking the net on you?

5. What are the three basic ingredients of a good serve?

6. Explain the statement, "Tennis matches are lost, not won."

7. Explain the following: 3 stroke game; 5 stroke game; all-court game.

8. List at least four strategies to use against two-handed players.

9. Describe at least six basic points of singles play strategy.

The Doubles Game

CHOOSING YOUR DOUBLES PARTNER

Playing doubles provides an opportunity to make many new friends. If, however, you are interested in playing serious long-term doubles, it would be wise to give some thought to picking your doubles partner. Some factors worthy of consideration are:

- Personality
- Type of game each partner plays (baseline or serve)
- Handedness of the partner. A right-hander and a left-hander make the strongest combination, since each has forehand crosscourt return of service.
- Strongest backhand usually plays the left court.

DOUBLES STRATEGY

The game of doubles is a team sport. Granted, there are only two members on the team, but when play begins, you are very much supportive of each other. There are several ways that singles and doubles differ.

1. The court is nine feet wider in doubles, bringing the alleys into use.
2. Both players share equal responsibility in covering court space.
3. General strategy involves both players going into the "attack" (net) position as quickly as possible and playing side by side.
4. You depend on your partner to adequately keep *you* out of trouble with his strokes and vice versa!
5. Ground strokes are less important. The serve, volley, return of service and overhead are the strokes most often used.
6. Placement of shots is more critical since an effort must be made to keep the ball away from the player(s) at the net.
7. Doubles is a much faster game, with drives being cut off by net volleys and sharp angles being hit.
8. A broader variety of strokes is used in doubles. Doubles players must practice all shots frequently.

Three types of doubles games are played today. They are basic doubles, Australian doubles and "club" or recreational doubles. These three vary in technique, court positions and strategy.

BASIC DOUBLES

Parallel Theory

Using the parallel theory, doubles partners play parallel to each other. They are responsible for covering all action in their respective halves of the court. Each partner is responsible for the area from the center service line to the doubles sideline and on their side from the baseline to the net. Often players feel they are responsible for "all the net" or "all the baseline." This would dictate an up and back position and would leave too much area open. In good doubles play, both players are "up and back" frequently, but always they play parallel to each other.

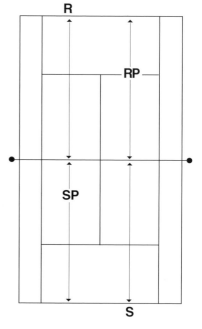

The diagram shows the basic doubles positions. The server (S) stands about three feet to the right of the center mark. The server's partner (SP) stands in the left service court, about four feet from the singles sideline and about six to eight feet from the net. The receiver (R) stands at the baseline awaiting the service. R should bisect the angle of the service. The receiver's partner (RP) stands on the service line. These basic positions are used to begin each point. From here the initial strategy begins and will depend on the knowledge and stroke production of the players involved.

As the service is made, the server moves up into the court, trying to get as close to the net as possible before the receiver returns the ball. Usually a step inside the service line is all that can be achieved, but this depends on the service and the speed of the server. As the service return passes over the net, the server uses a half-volley or a volley and progresses on in to establish a true net position. At this point, the server and partner are side by side, generally parallel to the net. Usually the receiver (R) will also move toward the net after the service is returned. The receiver's partner (RP) is stepping toward the net in an effort to cut off the volley. Frequently, all four players are at the net, looking for an opening to force an error or to hit a winner.

AUSTRALIAN DOUBLES

In this method of play, the RP is located as explained under parallel theory. The SP is now in the service court in front of the receiving net player. The server, upon delivering the service, must assume total responsibility for the returns coming "down the line" rather than crosscourt. This Aussie innovation will disturb those players accustomed to standard formations, but will not make a difference to good players. See diagrams below for court positions used in Australian doubles.

Points of Interest in Australian Doubles
1. Australian doubles are seldom used in good competition.
2. Australian doubles protects against a sharp crosscourt service return.
3. The receiver usually can easily return down the line.
4. The server must cover the alley frequently, thus eliminating the approach to the net.
5. The surprise element is good on occasion, if not overused.

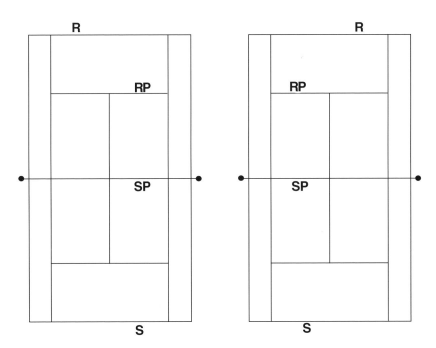

Australian Doubles: Forehand court   **Australian Doubles: Backhand court**

Doubles is a lifetime sport. The four players in this photo have 317 years of combined playing time.

CLUB OR RECREATIONAL DOUBLES

This style of play is worldwide in scope. It is recreational and is played for fun. However, the competitive instincts are still used and the desire to win is sometimes intense.

In club doubles, players usually do not have the stroke production or the physical prowess to play aggressive "basic" competitive doubles. In many instances, the footwork and hustle needed to get to the net are just not there. Also, it is not logical to follow a somewhat weak serve to the net.

Many players use a one-up, one-back formation. While this does not resemble two players in the center of the court in an "I" formation, it does have the basic characteristics of good doubles, even though neither the server nor the receiver makes any attempt to go to the net. Play is frequently between the server and receiver only, with an occasional lob causing the players to "switch" sides only to continue this basic style. It is very popular, comfortable, fun and within the general capabilities of most players.

Both players may stand anywhere on the court. Sometimes both players stay on the baseline, keeping the ball going back and forth using crosscourt drives and down the line shots.

The club style of play requires that certain principles be followed:
1. Serve to the weaker side of an opponent and deep into the service court.
2. Keep the ball in play.

3. Keep your return away from the net player.
4. If you lob, tell your partner.
5. If playing backcourt when your partner is at the net, cover lobs that go over his head. In other words, "switch" sides of the court.
6. Don't poach unless you can win the point.

By playing together frequently, teammates can easily complement each other, developing consistent placements, strategic volleys and accurate lobs. Then the team becomes hard to defeat.

TENNIS STRATEGY FOR DOUBLES

Good doubles is based on the server's being able to hold serve; that is, to win the game you are serving. To do this requires proper placement, spin and speed on the serve. Remember, it only takes one service break to win or lose a set.

Doubles strategy demands that the best server on your team should serve first in each set. It is easier to hold service with your stronger server. The server should consider the following points when serving:

1. Determine which side (forehand or backhand) your opponent has the most difficulty with in returning serve, then attack that side. This is generally the backhand side.
2. Find the serve (slice, twist or flat) that gives the receiver the most trouble. Go for that one frequently.
3. Look for an opening in the receiver's position. This creates a weak return.
4. Use enough speed on your serve to keep the receiver deep and protect your partner at the net.
5. Aim at the corners frequently to force a weak return.
6. Come to the net as often as possible.
7. Don't allow the opponent to anticipate your serves with regularity. Use variety.
8. Take your time on your serve.
9. Get your first serve in. It gives your team a great psychological advantage and your opponent will be deeper in his backcourt than on the second serve.
10. Use lots of spin on your second serve, but keep the opponent deep.
11. Let your partner try for any ball within reach. Do poach, whenever feasible.
12. Determine which player is the weaker, and play most of your shots to this opponent.
13. Arrange hand signals with your net partner so you will know his or her plans. Example—to poach or to stay? (See photos page 150).

I'm poaching   **I'm staying**

14. Increased spin allows more time to take the net.
15. A left-hander usually serves on the sunny side.
16. Angle is almost as important as speed, since it can pull the receiver wide and open the middle.
17. Never follow a weak serve to the net.
18. Get to the net quickly and often. The team at the net has a 90 percent chance of winning the point.
19. When both opponents are at the net, keep your shots down the middle and low. This often creates confusion as to who plays the ball and results in an error.
20. The three formations for doubles play are: (listed in order of importance):
    a. Both at the net: advanced, high intermediate
    b. Both at the baseline: beginner, intermediate
    c. One up, one back: beginner, intermediate
21. Remember to protect your partner at the net with good stroke execution. Follow these guidelines:
    a. Get the *first* serve in. Serve deep to the opponent's back-hand.
    b. Return deep to the crosscourt corner if the server doesn't come to the net. Attack the net with your partner immediately.
    c. Return the serve to the feet of the advancing server.
    d. Volley low so opponents must hit up on the ball.
    e. Lob deep over the head of the opposing net player.
    f. Drive down the alley if the opponent poaches early.

STRATEGY WHEN RECEIVING

Receiving serve is as important as serving. If you have a good service return you can break the opponents' serve and win a game. This takes practice and should become one of your most reliable strokes.

As in serving, returning the serve should be done with planning, care and deception. Variety is important, but not to the point that careless errors become rampant. Follow these guidelines for service returns:

1. **Place the ball in play.** It is imperative that the ball is placed in play each time your opponent serves. If nothing else, hack it back without trying to put special placement or spin on the ball. Do not defeat yourself. Make your opponent do it.

2. **Position for a return of service.** Bisect the angle between you and the server. That is, draw an imaginary line through the service area splitting the angle in an equal manner. You may be able to cheat on your opponent by slightly overplaying the backhand. Certainly, the opponent's serve should be tested to see if this can be done.

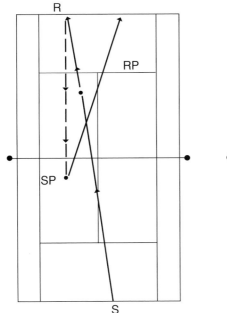

Classic Doubles Point #1:
S serves to R
R returns to SP
SP wins point with volley

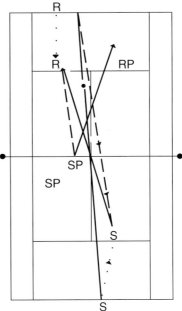

Classic Doubles Point #2:
S serves to R
R returns to S (moving in)
S returns to R (moving in)
R returns to SP (poaching)
SP volleys for a winner

3. **Be bouncy.** Worry your opponent. This does several things, it keeps you light on your feet and it distracts the server. This is particularly true if you walk up on the server's second serve just as the service is about to hit.

4. **Defensing the serve and volley.** Sometimes a chop or slice shot hit low and soft to an opponent's feet is very effective in countering the net rusher who likes to volley. If the ball is kept low at least your opponent cannot put it away but will have to volley up on the ball, thus allowing you an opportunity to put the next shot away.

5. **In general, do not lob a return of serve.** This is particularly true in singles. First, it is very difficult to lob a serve that has an excessive amount of spin. Second, a lob must be nearly perfect to be effective, and there is too much margin for error if this is not achieved. Even if it is a perfect lob, the opponent will usually have an opportunity to return the ball. Thus, you do not have a clear winner.

6. If the server has an extremely fast serve and you are playing on a hard surface, it is probably better to return service one or two steps behind the baseline. However, with most tennis players, it is generally a good idea to return the first serve from near the baseline and to move in one or two steps for the second serve.

7. If an opponent is consistently winning the serve, change your procedures. Whatever you are doing, do something different.

8. **Play percentages.** Use your percentage return. Hit the shot that will most often place the ball in play.

9. When returning serve, try to return it as deep as possible. The best place is one to two feet inside the baseline, preferably to the opponents' weak side.

10. If the opponent is consistently scoring on the serve, **change the target.** Move in very close, overplay on one side or the other, but change the target so your opponent is not looking at the same target each time.

11. Some players grow accustomed to having an opponent play on or near the baseline. Thus, when the opponent moves in extremely close, they will usually try to put more spin or speed on the ball and frequently lose their effectiveness on the first serve.

12. Always remember that tennis is a game of percentages. To be a winner, you must hit shots that give you the best return percentage and not hit those shots that are less productive or prone to error.

13. If you are most effective from the baseline, then you should not take the net unless forced to do so. Conversely, if your opponent does not lob well and you have the good volley then attack at every opportunity.

14. If an opponent gives even the slightest indication that he or she dislikes one of your shots (for example, a drop shot, since some players are very lazy), then keep chipping away.

15. In general, return a drop shot with a drop shot, since most players retreat to the baseline after hitting a drop shot.
16. Most shots that are missed as a player rushes the net are hit long, because the average player does not compensate for forward body momentum.
17. Remember that your partner is moving toward the net on your service return. If you are missing shots, check your fundamentals: footwork, eye on the ball, turning the side and good stroke production. Stay with basic tennis strategy. Rarely vary from it. And... IT WORKS!!

USE OF THE VOLLEY, SMASH AND LOB

In doubles, the initial alignment of players, both in serving and receiving, indicates a strong emphasis toward establishing an attack position at the net. The volley, the smash and the lob become most important. The volley and/or the lob assist with attempts to get to the net. Once there, the overhead smash helps win points.

Following is a brief review of these three strokes as they pertain to basic doubles strategy.

The Volley. This stroke is an offensive weapon, used in attempts to win the point by an angle or to force a weak return. On the serving side, the server's partner is already established at the net hoping to cut off a drive and win the point. The server will serve and come to the net, often using the volley to get there.

At the net, the volley is used to win the point. The receiving team is positioned to take the net position if the serving team doesn't beat them to it. The receiver's partner is at the service line ready to come in and the receiver, if the server doesn't come in, should return deep and approach the net. The volley is the basic point winner as both players are at the net.

The Smash. The smash wins the point quicker and more often than the volley. However, to use a smash, an opponent must hit a lob that is short enough for smash execution. This can usually be done by a forcing ground stroke, service or volley. Since everyone will be playing at the net, all doubles participants should have a good overhead.

The Lob. This is the most under-used shot in tennis. However, if executed properly, it can be devastating. In doubles, opponents will attack the net; this makes them vulnerable to the lob. Proper use of the lob causes them to be pushed back from the attack position into a defensive position at the baseline. Also, if your lob is to their backhand and has some topspin, you can easily attack behind this shot.

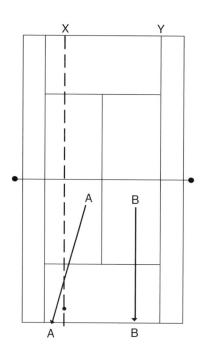

Covering the Lob: Using the parallel theory of coverage, each player covers all shots (lobs included) on his side. In this diagram, X lobs deep behind A, who easily retreats and covers the return.

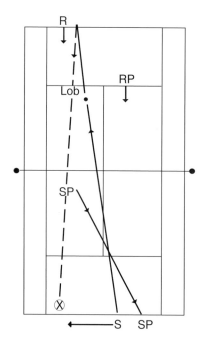

Covering the Lob:
Server covers the lob.
SP covers open area.
R and RP move to the net.

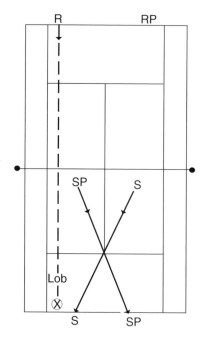

Covering the Lob:
S and SP both at the net.
S takes the lob.
SP covers the open court.

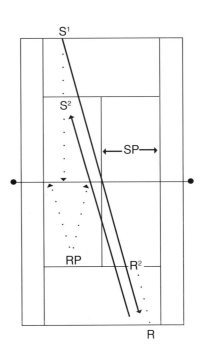

Court positions of advanced players and net positions after serving and receiving. Both are on the attack and try to achieve the net position. Volley and half-volley are usually used.

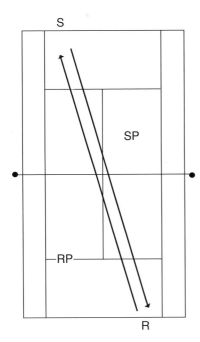

Comparison for club doubles using the one up and one back system. Play is directed S to R and so forth. S and R cover all deep shots to either side, with no poaching by either SP or RP. R and S maintain positions at the baseline; RP and SP maintain forward positions.

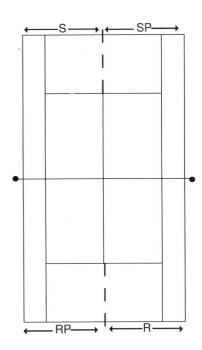

Positions for beginner doubles. Both players maintain positions at the baseline on each side. Each player is responsible for his half of the court and rarely advances to the net. Most points are won on errors rather than placements.

Doubles is a great game. Unlike singles, teamwork is involved. Good players complement each other. However, partners must know basic strategy and have good execution of fundamentals. Partners must understand what is expected insofar as serving, receiving, net play, court coverage and teamwork. Once you get into the game, you'll find great enjoyment in this new-found challenge. It can last a lifetime!

CANADIAN DOUBLES

A unique system of play called Canadian Doubles is sometimes found at recreation areas and clubs. This game uses three players instead of the normal number of four for doubles play. Canadian doubles is not an official game and should be used for fun and recreation only.

In Canadian doubles, a single person plays two opponents. The singles player must cover the singlets court only, while the two opponents must cover their doubles court. Rules of tennis are followed for the singles and doubles players with regard to their court area of coverage.

Since this is not a recognized system of singles or doubles, fun is the main attraction. The game is an alternative method of play when short one player.

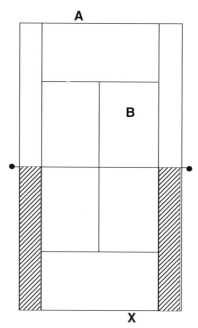

A and B cover the doubles court; X covers only the singles court (the alleys are not used).

QUESTIONS AND ANSWERS ABOUT DOUBLES

How can I improve my doubles game quickly?
There is no such thing as quick success in tennis; however, concentrate on the following to improve your doubles game:
1. Keep the ball low when hitting from the baseline, and when in trouble, aim just above the net strap.
2. Take the serve sooner. Move in or up to return first and second serves. Chip the return and take the net.
3. Improve your serve, return of serve, volley and lob.
4. Know your partner and communicate.

Should the less skillful partner play the backhand or forehand court?
Since the important points are most often played in the backhand court, generally the best player should be in that position. This usually places the strongest forehand guarding the middle and the strongest overhead in a high percentage position.

What should I do if I am continually harassed and intimidated by anyone who poaches on me?
An aggressive poacher can frequently win more points by causing opponent errors than by actually putting the ball away. The first thing to do is keep the poacher anchored. This is best achieved with a sharp shot to the body. A down-the-line shot is good, but your percentage decreases on this shot. The two safest shots are the sharp-angled return and the lob. The lob is particularly good in doubles if the server is coming in behind the serve, and the poacher is playing close to the net as poachers usually do.

Why am I not winning points by poaching?
You are probably poaching on the wrong shots. Look for the slice or chop returns that have a tendency to rise and float. You might also be letting the ball drop from its high point after crossing the net. The offensive volley is a high to low shot and the higher the impact point above the net, the better. Also, contact the ball in front of the body.

What can I do when my partner will not take advantage of an opponent's weak second serve and advance to the net?
Under normal circumstances you should both be on the net at every opportunity. However, if your opponents are regularly lobbing over you or your partner's head and you can't handle the shot, or if both volleys are not strong, then it might be better to lay back more.

Why do I get caught flat-footed on hard serves and some wide balls?
One way to speed up your reaction time is to bounce-hop most of the time. Keep your feet in motion but close to the ground.

I am getting passed down my alley too often. Any advice?
Even great poachers sometimes get passed. You might try faking but not going a little more often. If you are still being passed then you are either thinking about something else or your partner is setting you up.

I have a doubles partner who loves to poach and is good at it, but has a tendency to return to his original spot. We frequently both end up on the same side of the court. Any advice?
This can be a problem, but a simple hand signal behind the back helps keep the backcourt person informed. Another simple rule that helps is whenever a ball passes by or over a net person, that person should immediately move to the other side of the court. Also, anyone crossing the center line on a poach, successful or otherwise, should never return to the original side until after the point has been concluded.

What about a left-hander, right-hander combination team?
Logically, the lefty should play the deuce court because most of the shots will go down the middle. However, two examples of great doubles teams having the lefty playing the add court are Martina Navratilova and Pam Shriver, and John McEnroe and Peter Fleming.

Who takes a ball coming down the middle when two players are at the net?
Here are five options:
1. The last person to hit the ball plays the return shot because that player is more likely to be focused on the next shot.
2. The partner with the strongest shot takes it.
3. The player closest to the net takes the shot.
4. The player diagonally opposite from the opponent who hit the last shot plays the ball. The reasoning for this is that this move should free your partner to better protect the alley. Or if your opponents try a sharply angled crosscourt volley, you merely have to move in to put the ball away. You should also have an easier time reaching the shot because it will be returning from crosscourt.
5. The player with the forehand shot takes the ball for the return.

Chapter 12: Evaluation

1. Why is the volley more important in doubles than singles?

2. How would you attack an Australian doubles formation?

3. Why is the choice of a doubles partner so important?

4. List five basic responsibilities that are important when playing club style (one up/one back) doubles.

5. Define "Canadian Doubles."

6. Explain the concept that ground strokes are less important in doubles than singles.

7. If your serving partner fails to take the net, what should you attempt to do?

8. Why is the lob more important in doubles play than in singles play?

9. Why is poaching so important to good doubles play?

10. Why should the best server on a team generally serve first?

Chapter 13

Conditioning for Tennis

Perhaps the first question that needs to be asked is "Why do I want or need to be stronger?" If you aspire to be a tennis player, strength is an asset.

Evidence suggests that stronger muscles protect the joints, thereby decreasing joint injuries. Muscles with greater strength and endurance are less susceptible to sprains, strains and tears. Another added benefit is that better muscle tone of the trunk muscles decreases the likelihood of lower back pain and weak, sagging abdominals.

Additional reasons for maintaining good muscular strength and endurance are less susceptibility to fatigue, faster rehabilitation of muscle injury, increased feelings of self-confidence and improved outlook. A complete fitness base for tennis requires both aerobic as well as anaerobic stamina. A tennis workout program needs to include wind sprints designed to improve an athlete's ability to recover from a long point. It also needs to include shorter sprints and quick side to side movements in order to improve lateral movements and quickness to the ball. A tennis player should train to be able to run at full speed for 6-8 seconds for a long period of time. A fitness program with only long distance running or only short sprints and strength work will not properly prepare the player for long matches. It is the combination of this work that will create the complete tennis fitness base.

An example of a weekly fitness schedule on top of tennis practice may look like this:

Day 1 (Monday): Linear day. Wind sprints 4-8 sets of 5 50 yard sprints with 10 seconds rest in between sprints and 90 seconds in between sets.

Day 2 (Wednesday): Lateral day. On court quickness drills with or without a tennis ball designed to enhance lateral movement and recovery to the middle. These drills are also run in sets with set recovery times in between each repetition and set.

Day 3 (Friday): Miscellaneous day. A workout that incorporates both lateral and linear speed.

CONDITIONING EXERCISES

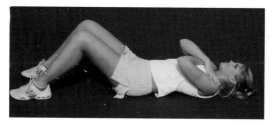

QUESTIONS AND ANSWERS ABOUT CONDITIONING

What makes a person a champion or an all-star?
The great Vince Lombardi once said, "Success happens when preparation meets opportunity." Today's athletes are performing on a much higher level than ever before, because they and their coaches are working harder to achieve perfection.

Could you provide some suggestions for mapping out practice sessions like college players do?
During the off-season months (if there are any) most college players use the weight room to develop strength and endurance. In-season practice sessions usually include stretching exercises, warm-up stroke practice, stroke drills, competitive drills, match practice, cool-down stretching and jogging or running. The amount of time you devote to each area depends on your needs.

What is the best way to replace the fluids lost playing tennis?
Water remains the number one choice. For endurance events lasting longer than 60 minutes, a diluted (5-8 percent carbohydrate) drink is useful. Carbohydrates delay the beginning symptoms of exhaustion. The rule of thumb is to drink fluids equal in volume to that lost by sweating; sixteen fluid ounces are generally considered to be equal to one pound. If your stomach can handle it, you might try a mixture of tomato juice and water. Both absorb quickly and the tomato juice has some potassium and sodium, which will help replace that lost and perhaps delay the onset of muscle cramping.

Can dehydration cause poor play?
A recent study involved 12 members of the U.S. Junior Wightman Cup team. After five days of training at the Colorado Springs Olympic Training Camp, several had lost more than seven pounds of water and were approximately 3.75 percent dehydrated. Since a two percent level of dehydration affects reaction time, speed and concentration, their performance was definitely below par. Each felt, however, that she was adequately replacing her daily water loss.

Is there any harm in grunting when hitting the ball?
Excessive grunting can cause symptoms of hyperventilation. The release of too much carbon dioxide causes difficulty in breathing, numbness in hands, muscle tightening and sometimes chest pain. If you experience these symptoms, try breathing in and out of a closely-held paper bag.

Can tennis prevent osteoporosis (loss of bone mass)?
When bone does not experience normal stress through inactivity, it begins to deteriorate. Research, as reported by Shaler, Steel and Carter at Stanford University, indicates that "for bone mass maintenance, it is much more important to have activities with high loads and high stresses than activities with lots of cycles." If they are correct, then tennis should build bone mass. Of course, proper blood calcium levels are necessary.

How serious is the threat of skin cancer to tennis players? Is there a certain area or body part that is most susceptible?
The threat is very serious. This year about 700,000 new cases of skin cancer will be diagnosed by doctors. The world's ozone layer decreased five percent in the 1980s, and for every decrease in the ozone layer there is a corresponding increase in skin cancer cases. Everyone is at risk, especially outdoor tennis players. Approximately 80 percent of all skin cancers occur on the hands and face.

What should be used to block the sun's rays?
There are two basic kinds of lotions, sunscreens and sun blocks. Sunscreens filter the sun's rays while sun blocks block all rays from the sun. Some lotions are classified as "waterproof" and some are "water resistant." Read the bottle carefully to determine under what conditions and for what length of time the lotion will protect. Since tennis players sweat heavily and some matches last several hours, you may need to reapply your choice.

How important is physical fitness to good health?
While good health and physical fitness are related, regular physical activity does produce some health benefits that are not directly related to a high degree of physical fitness. Some research studies among adults have shown that exercise on a regular basis is directly related to reduced cases of mental health problems (depression), diabetes, osteoporosis, and certain types of cancer. That regular low-intensity exercise can provide some protection has been further documented by Pfaffenbarger and others in their Harvard alumni study and by Laporte's group of researchers.

How good is tennis as a fitness activity?
It depends on the duration and intensity of play. Playing singles for at least 30 minutes three times per week against a player equal to or better than yourself, can improve cardiovascular fitness. Some call this "aerobic tennis," and working the body at this level can:
- raise the HDL (that's the "good" kind) cholesterol level and lower the total cholesterol level

- help to control weight
- lower blood pressure
- relieve psychological stress

What is the relationship between percentage of body fat and very good tennis players?

Most very good tennis players are not fat. A study of United States, English and Swedish teenage tournament players by Dr. Ben Kibler, a member of the USTA Sport Science Advisory Council, found the boys' body fat range to be 15-18 percent while the girls' values were from 18-25 percent. Top male adult players carry about 15 percent.

Are carbohydrates important to a person who engages in heavy exercise?

Yes. The average American athlete probably consumes 40 to 45 percent of daily calories from fat. Most trainers now recommend that athletes eat about 70 percent of total calories in the form of carbohydrates. This serves two important purposes: First, it reduces cholesterol intake. Second, high carbohydrate diets are especially important when training or competing on successive days.

If I do cheat a little on my diet, which food would hurt me least?

As Socrates once said, "Moderacy in all things." A little cheating probably won't hurt at all. Sugar is probably the least harmful substance for an active tennis player. High-fat foods and excessive protein are probably the worst. High-fat foods produce too much cholesterol and decrease the body's oxygen delivery capability. Excessive protein causes an over accumulation of uric acid and dehydration. Salt could be a problem if you are bothered by high blood pressure.

How many calories does a person need each day?

You might follow this simple guideline. Find the category that best describes your activity level to determine how many calories per pound of body weight should be consumed to remain the same weight.

- **Very active:** 25 calories per pound of body weight
- **Moderately active:** 20 calories per pound of body weight
- **Lightly Active:** 15 calories per pound of body weight
- **Very inactive:** 10-12 calories per pound of body weight

Remember that while total calories are important, a balanced diet is probably more important to all-around total health.

Are there any foods that cause the body to burn more calories?

No. However, there are foods that can help cut down caloric consumption. One Pennsylvania study indicated that people who eat more soup lose more weight. The study found that those who ate soup less than four times per week had a weight loss average of 15 percent of excess weight. Eating soup four or more times per week had a weight loss average of 20 percent of excess weight.

Another study at Baylor College of Medicine found that soup eaters were more likely to maintain their weight loss after one year. The two factors contributing to the effectiveness of soup are its lower caloric density and the length of time it takes to consume it, particularly if hot.

Is playing tennis a good way to burn calories?

The number of calories burned is related to how many pounds you are pushing around the court, how much distance you travel, your level of play and the length of your rallies. On the average, a woman will expend 400 calories per hour playing singles, while a man will burn about 600. Doubles play reduces expenditures for both men and women to about two-thirds of this number.

What do you recommend for a pre-match meal?

There is no magic pregame meal. Most experts agree that the pregame meal should be low in fat and protein, non-bulky and high in complex carbohydrates.

How long should the warm-up take?

A warm-up should allow a person to operate at 100 percent efficiency before playing the first point. The time will vary with each person, but usually there is a feeling of well-being and readiness as the warm-up progresses. You should be ready when you break into a good sweat. The amount of time that it takes to do this depends on the temperature, the humidity and the intensity of your warm-up.

What changes should be made when warming-up on a cold day?

Stretching cold muscles on a cold day sometimes causes injuries. Do some very light exercises to warm the muscles. Then do your stretching.

What can be done to prevent muscle pulls and tears?

It is possible to pull muscles just by stretching. Players who are susceptible to pulls and tears should try raising the body's temperature before stretching exercises. Pile on a few extra layers of clothing or take a hot shower or both before doing warm-up exercises.

How can I make my muscles grow?

Muscle growth depends on three things.

1. Growth stimulation must occur within the body at the basic cellular level. After puberty, this is accomplished by high-intensity exercise.

2. Proper nutrients must be available for the stimulated cells. Providing large amounts of nutrients in excess of what the body requires does nothing to promote the growth of muscle fibers. The growth machinery within the cell must be turned on. Muscle stimulation must always precede nutrition. If you stimulate muscular growth by high-intensity exercise, then your muscles will grow on almost any reasonable diet.

3. Adequate rest is needed to allow the body time to repair cell damage and to replace the muscle tissue rebuilding ingredients. The chemical reactions inside a growing muscle are much more complicated than just exercising, eating and resting. High-intensity muscular contractions result in the formation of a chemical called creatine. This, in turn, causes the muscle to form more myosin, which enables it to undergo stronger contractions. This, in turn, causes the production of more creatine.

Remember, stimulate muscle growth through high-intensity exercise and then provide the proper nutrients and rest.

Should tennis players cross train?

Cross training, the use of other sports or activities to develop the body for a particular sport, has revolutionized racket sports. Serious tennis and racquetball players have reduced their court time to three or four hours per day. More emphasis is devoted to cardiovascular conditioning and upper body and leg strength. Cross training provides variety for serious tennis players. Don't be afraid to become involved in other athletic endeavors that will help you play to your peak performance.

Shoulder stretch

What is the most common injury among tennis players?

While many part-time players frequently report elbow and forearm injuries, Dr. Kibler believes that rotator cuff (shoulder) tendonitis is the most common injury among tournament grade players. He believes the key to preventing this injury is to increase the shoulder's ability to stretch. The application of excessive topspin, requiring violent low to high shoulder motion, may contribute to rotator cuff problems. (See photo for exercise to increase stretching ability.)

What is tennis elbow?

Physicians say there are two types: lateral (outside) and medial (inside) with the outside kind being about five times more common. Tennis elbow is created by microscopic tears in the muscles and tendons that control the wrist and fingers. The site of pain is where the tendons attach in the elbow. Causes are generally poor technique and/or overuse. Other possibilities include playing with tight strings, wet and heavy tennis balls, and/or excessively heavy or light tennis rackets. The poor technique that often causes this injury is leading with the elbow. Use rest, ice and aspirin or other over-the-counter medications to treat the pain.

How prevalent is tennis elbow?

One study, as reported by *Tennis* magazine, indicated that 20 percent of surveyed respondents had elbow problems. Most were using a lightweight racket at the time of injury. Players suffering with tennis elbow should probably avoid the very stiff rackets such as graphite, boron and steel. If the elbow is extremely bad, a wood racket may be best.

Conditioning Exercises

COMMON TENNIS INJURIES

Sprained Ankle

Ankle sprains are one of the most common tennis injuries. The injury usually involves damage to ligaments and tendons surrounding the joint and/ or to the capsule-like sac surrounding the joint. Severe ankle sprains may not be distinguishable from a fracture (except by x-ray) and may take longer to heal. However, there are procedures that, if followed, will minimize pain and speed recovery.

1. Stop activity—take weight off foot.
2. Elevate leg and apply an elastic (Ace) bandage, taking care that you do not apply the bandage so tightly that circulation to the foot is cut off.
3. Apply ice water or cold packs until swelling is stabilized.

Restoration of flexibility should begin after the damaged ligaments, tendons and capillaries have healed. Begin by moving the ankle through its entire range of motion several times daily. Applying pressure with the side of your foot to a chair helps. Later, try filling a sock with sand and placing it across the foot before doing a wide range of motion.

Taping or wrapping before the ankle strength is fully restored is usually a sound preventive measure. However, after full recovery, most authorities recommend removal of supports so that a full strengthening of the limb can occur.

Blisters

Tennis is a game of sudden starts and stops. This entails great wear and tear on the feet and frequently results in blisters. Preseason jogging, wearing two pairs of socks, keeping the feet dry and wearing properly fitted shoes helps prevent the problem. When a blister does occur there are two choices: (1) Leave it alone and the fluids will eventually be absorbed by the body. (2) Scrub thoroughly with soap and water, then sterilize a needle over an open flame and make a small opening at the base or back part of the blister. Drain the fluid and apply a sterile dressing. If you must continue to play, a small felt or sponge rubber pad with a hole (doughnut) cut in the center will offer some protection by taking the pressure off that particular spot. If you are prone to hand blisters, they can sometimes be prevented by using a tennis glove.

Muscle Cramps

Cramps are sudden involuntary muscle contractions causing great pain. They may occur at any time and are characterized by repeated contractions and relaxations or sometimes as a steady continuous muscle contraction. Their causes are varied; however, fatigue, loss of body fluids and minerals, and the accumulation of waste products within the muscles are all contributing factors. Rest and replenishment of body fluids and salts will usually remedy the problem.

Muscle Pulls and Tears

This disability is usually caused by lack of flexibility and excessive stress. One of the most common muscle tears occurs in the calf muscle. When this injury occurs, there is immediate sharp pain within the heavy part of the calf. Swelling usually occurs within a few hours and the area may become black and blue within several days. Walking, running or rising on the toes is painful. Immediate application of cold packs and resting the leg usually helps. Later, applications of moist heat, massage and gradual usage will hasten recovery.

Back Pain

Back pain is a reasonably common occurrence among part-time and full-time athletes. The most common cause is postural—i.e., shortened hamstring and back muscles accompanied by weak abdominal muscles. Bent knee sit-ups accompanied by stretching exercises for the back and hamstring muscles usually prevent or lessen this injury. Once back pain occurs, the best treatment is rest. Application of heat sometimes helps but application must be limited to small amounts of time at a low setting. Too much heat will increase irritation and swelling, thus causing more pain. Do not fall asleep on a heating pad.

Chapter 13: Evaluation

1. What is necessary to stimulate muscle growth?

2. List things you should do as a warm-up prior to a tough tennis match.

3. What should you immediately do if you pull a muscle during a tennis match?

4. What is the best way to reduce or prevent muscle cramping?

5. What should you do if you sprain your ankle on the tennis court?

6. Explain the concept that tennis is a "fitness" activity.

7. What can be done to help prevent foot blisters?

8. In most tournaments the warm-up time is five minutes. How will you handle this when a normal warm-up period is much longer?

Chapter 14
Practice Drills

Tennis drills should be progressive. There are no shortcuts for learning skill patterns. A student should seek professional instruction, which will set the pace, determine the course, and generate interest in achieving one's potential. The tennis instructor should establish drills and patterns for practice. Many of these drills will be "dry" drills, using no balls but simply going through the stroking pattern, to learn the sequence and to train the muscles in acquiring new skills.

Practically speaking, drills are divided into four general areas:

1. Footwork drills
2. Basic instructional drills
3. Skill drills
4. Advanced competitive drills

SELECTED FOOTWORK DRILLS

Because footwork is about 60 percent of the game, this fundamental must be developed to the maximum level. The following footwork patterns have been selected because of their aggressiveness, practicality and conditioning benefits. No balls are hit in any of these footwork drills.

Jump rope: Use primarily a single hop; may be done using both feet together, or alternating feet. Jumping rope is also useful as a conditioner. Several patterns and styles can be used.

Crossover step: Punch volley each step. Begin in a ready position, then use a cross-step (forward pivot) to the forehand and to the backhand in quick repetition, hitting an imaginary volley each time. Emphasize speed and correct footwork pattern. Do four to six thirty-second rounds.

Serve and go: Begin at the baseline, without use of tennis balls. Serve and go to the net, using a check stop at the service line and continuing to the net. Repeat many times.

Zigzag run: From center mark, place balls in an irregular pattern on either side. Using a broken pattern, proceed to each ball on the ground and stroke each imaginary ball at the location of the ball on the ground.

Up the alley: Using the cross-step pattern already described, begin at the baseline on one side of the alley. Use the pattern to cross and punch an imaginary volley, continuing to move forward each step. Continue until you go "up the alley." Execution should be rapid and footwork should be correct. Do approximately six rounds.

Up and over: Start at the singles sideline. Move forward to the service line then stop and hit an imaginary ground stroke, then go along the service line to the midcourt line, stop and hit a ground stroke, go up the midcourt line to the net, punch a volley, then go to the side—right or left—extend (stretch) to hit the final volley. Go to the opposite side of the baseline and begin again. Go through five times.

Side step drill: Start halfway between the midcourt line and singles sideline. Using a side skipping motion, move to a point that allows you to stroke a ball at the singles sideline, pivot and stroke. Rapidly recover and move to the midcourt line and execute a stroke, repeat for 30 seconds. Start again. Continue for four to six repetitions.

Jog and stroke: Starting at court #1 on your court complex, jog around the courts. Check stop every five steps and stroke a forehand or a backhand, alternating with each stop. Continue around the courts.

Shuttle run: Place four balls on the court equidistant from the baseline to the net. Begin by running, racket in hand, to the first ball, return to the baseline running backwards, then go to the second ball. Continue to the baseline backwards, then on to the third, etc., until you go to all four balls. Repeat three times.

Quick step and volley: Spread out on the court. Run in place. On every tenth step quickly execute a forehand volley, recover and continue to run in place; then hit a backhand volley. Continue this routine for thirty seconds or more. This can be done easily with a partner using hand signals—move to the side according to whether partner quickly lifts right or left arm. Be alert. Move the feet at all times.

Sundial: From your position on the court, place seven balls eight feet from you, representing the hours on the face of a clock. Step and stretch to reach each ball, using correct footwork for the side of the body on which the ball is located.

BASIC INSTRUCTIONAL DRILLS

The Forehand

Repetitions	Individual drills
10	1. From a ready position, assume the shake hands grip. Release, repeat.
10	2. From a ready position, try the forward pivot, check foot position, recover.
10	3. Repeat #2 using the reverse pivot.
10	4. Using the forward pivot, take the complete backswing. Check height of the racket hand.
10	5. Using the forward pivot, combine the backswing, forward swing and follow-through in one smooth, flowing motion.
25	6. From the back of the court, turn your left side to the fence. Drop a ball in front of the left side and stroke it into the fence 20 feet away. Recover to the ready position, then repeat. Now hit the ball over the net.
25	7. Drop a ball as in #6 and stroke it to a rebound wall. Catch ball, drop and repeat.
20	8. Repeat #7, keep the ball to the right half of the forward rebound wall and above the three-foot net line.
20	9. Repeat #8, keeping the ball in play to the right half of the forward rebound wall.
30	10. Try to replay the rebound against the forward wall (number of bounces is not important at this stage).

Repetitions	Partner drills
30	11. Have a partner toss from the net (center) to a circle just behind the service line. Stroke using full pivot.
30	12. Toss from net into a circle just above the baseline, stroke from baseline into opponent's court. Use full pivot.
3	13. Repeat #12, except substitute a ball machine for tosser. Hit three baskets of balls each.
3	14. Repeat #13. Aim each ball to the opposite side of opponent's court from the last ball (check fundamentals).
30 min.	15. Drop a ball and stroke to your partner on the opposite side of the net. Try to continue a forehand rally.

If you detect any trouble with the forehand, go back and review the fundamentals. Acquire a good mental picture of the proper form. Understanding it will greatly assist in skill development.

As with the forehand, the drills listed below are in progressive order from the simple to the complex. Use these drills slowly, taking time to practice each step thoroughly before continuing. The number of repetitions is a guide only. An individual may need fewer or more depending on personal progress.

The Backhand

Repetitions	Individual drills
10	1. From a ready position, change from a forehand to a backhand grip.
10	2. Repeat #1 and use the forward pivot to the left side changing grips as you execute the pivot. Check foot-work positions.
10	3. Repeat #2 and use the reverse pivot, stepping back rather than forward.
10	4. Using the forward pivot, take the racket back to the full backswing position. Check the height of racket head (keep low).
15	5. Repeat #4 and add the forward swing and follow-through. Go very slowly, check racket head position. Lead with the head of racket.
25	6. From the back of the court area turn your right side to the fence, drop a ball in front of the right side and execute a backhand stroke to the fence, 20 feet away. Recover and repeat.
25	7. Drop a ball and stroke it to a rebound wall. Catch the ball and repeat.
25	8. Repeat #7, except aim the ball above an imaginary three-foot line representing the tennis net.
20	9. Repeat #8, keeping the ball to the left side of the front wall.
20	10. Try to replay the rebound against the forward wall (number of bounces is not important now).

Repetitions	Partners drills
30	11. Have a partner toss from the center of the net into a small circle behind the service line. Stroke, using a full backhand with pivot, adjusting the toss to the circle.
30	12. Toss from the net into a circle just above the baseline. Stroke from the baseline into the opponent's court. Use full pivot.
3+	13. Repeat #12, except substitute ball machine for tosser. Hit at least three trays of balls each.

The Backhand *(cont.)*

Repetitions	Partners drills
3	14. Repeat #13, aim each ball to the opposite side of opponent's court from the last ball. Check fundamentals.
30 min.	15. Drop a ball and stroke to your partner on the opposite side to the net. Try to continue a backhand rally.
	16. Using both forehand and backhand, drop a ball and keep a rally going as long as possible. Continue until the continuous count totals 1,000 shots hit over the net.

You have now completed drills for the two basic tennis strokes. If there is a problem, question or concern, contact your instructor or go back and read and repeat your skill progressions. When you have completed the work on the backhand stroke, review the skill and knowledge objectives to determine if further emphasis is needed.

The Service

Repetitions	Drills
20	1. Practice the coordination of swing for both arms. Right arm to backswing and left arm toward ball toss. Shift weight back as arms begin movement. Do not toss the ball.
30	2. Practice the toss, noticing the ball's height and where it lands on the court.
25	3. Repeat #1, tossing ball up as racket arm is taken back. Do not hit the ball.
30	4. Repeat #3. Face the fence, and serve into the fence, work on ball toss, contact point and height.
5	5. At service line, serve five good serves to the correct service court.[1]
5+	6. Repeat #5, except move back one yard after each five good serves, gradually working towards the baseline.
20+	7. From the baseline, using correct form, hit ten serves to right court, then ten to left court. Repeat.
20	8. Serve 20 flat serves into the right service court.
20	9. Serve 20 flat serves into the left service court.
200	10. Serve 100 balls to each service court, right and left.
	11. Divide the opposite service courts into quarters. Serve 25 balls to each area.

---

[1] If a full swing is difficult, use a half-swing motion, beginning with the racket in the "behind the back" position.

The Service *(cont.)*

Repetitions	Drills
	Area #1: Forehand corner for receiver, *Right service court*
	Area #2: Backhand corner for receiver, *Right service court*
	Area #3: Forehand corner for receiver, *Left service court*
	Area #4: Backhand corner for receiver, *Left service court*
	As you continue to practice, aim the ball to either area 1 or 2, or area 3 or 4, depending on which side you are serving from. Always serve diagonally across the court.
200	12. Repeat #10, but serve 50 serves to each area (1-4) in numerical order.

Increase speed only when able to maintain control and placement.

The Volley

Repetitions	Drills
30	1. From proper net position, have partner toss balls to your forehand, from service line. Volley back to your partner. Keep toss chest high, throw overhand.
30	2. Repeat #1, using the backhand volley.
50	3. Alternating forehand and backhand volley, hit from toss back to partner. Toss overhand.
50	4. Forehand only, vary height of the toss. Direct volley toward partner if possible.
30	5. Repeat #4 using the backhand.
30	6. Repeat #3; aim ball to opposite corner of opponent's court.
30	7. Repeat #4; aim ball to opposite corner of opponent's court.
4	8. Using a ball machine, alternate loads to the forehand and backhand, two rounds of balls to each side.
20	9. Using the same machine, from the same tossing position move from the baseline, stroking the ball to the opponent's backhand; move to the net and volley the next ball. (Repeat: 10 approach shots and 10 volleys.)
20	10. Have baseline partner stroke a ball to you at the net, then volley the ball back to partner for another ground stroke. Feed the ball to each other.

The Smash

Repetitions	Drills
10	1. Assume the correct grip, turn to the left side of the net in the forecourt area and exercise the full swing without the ball.
30	2. Toss from the baseline to the partner at the net (fore-court). Smash the ball at half speed into the opponent's court.
20	3. Repeat #2, but begin aiming the ball at different angles (left, right, short, deep).
20	4. Repeat #2, but aim the ball to the opponent's deep backcourt area.
20	5. Have partner lob the ball to you using a racket. Execute the smash to varying areas of opponent's courts.

SKILL DRILLS

Most skill drills are part of an intensive practice plan. There are drills for each stroke, often using a partner to feed the ball. It is good practice for both players. Three drill areas are basic to good tennis and should be practiced regularly.
These are:
1. Serve and return of serve
2. Ground stroke consistency and accuracy from the baseline
3. Placement of passing shots

Additional time should be given to the accomplishment of the support strokes, or those which complement the basic game.
These are:
1. Serve and volley combination
2. The approach shot
3. Volley and net tactics
4. The overhead or smash
5. Offensive and defensive lobs

Allow time for practice and play, with neither partner totally dominating the other. Some selected skill drills are as follows:
1. Rally from the backcourt area at the center mark.
2. Stroke crosscourt shots—both backhand and forehand rallies.
3. Use an "X" drill. One partner hits crosscourt only, while the other partner hits down the line only.

4. Two partners face each other near the sideline. One hits forehands down the line and the partner hits backhands. To include a footwork drill, move from the center mark to the sideline. One partner works on forehand, the other on backhand.

5. One partner has a basket of balls at service line. Hit balls to partner, running partner from corner to corner.

6. Serve only—to both forehand and backhand service courts.

7. One partner at the net, one at the baseline—rally.

8. Same as #7, using only forehand or only backhand.

9. One partner at net, one at baseline, volley and lob practice.

10. Using a feeder, hit forehand or backhand volleys only.

11. Overheads, feed setups from the baseline.

12. Volley-rally-overhead drill. One partner at the net, other at the baseline. The net player hits a volley from the drive and then the overhead fed by the baseliner.

13. Hit overhead, touch net, hit overhead, and touch net; continue 10 times. Feeder is partner at the baseline, who only feeds.

14. Four-ball drill: Hit from baseline, half-volley at service line, volley at net and overhead. Feeder is partner at the baseline.

15. Serve and lob return drill. Basic practice for doubles, good change of pace drill.

16. Serve or return serve to target area. Use tennis balls or cans as targets. Player A can practice serves—player B, returns, change.

17. Angled volley to backhand cones—either side. Feeder at center of baseline. Basket of balls to each partner. Feeder may move along baseline to create different angles.

18. Both partners at net—volley from the service line, keeping the ball in play.

19. Same as #18 only use crosscourt volley.

20. Volley rally against a wall. Try "no bounce allowed."

21. Three-player volley drill: All players at the service line, keeping one ball in play. Change places frequently.

22. "X" drill with one player at the net volleying crosscourt only, while partner at the baseline hits ground strokes down the line only. Both players keep ball within reach of partner but require extensive movement. May vary at random.

COMPETITIVE DRILLS

These drills may use a point system to encourage a game-like situation. Practice should be intense and care should be taken not to make careless errors. Most drills are aggressive and demand skill competency.

Serve and return of serve: One player serves only, and the partner works on service returns only. Vary serves and returns, concentrating on effective strategy. Alternate using both courts and rotate players.

Serve and play out point: The server moves into net and the players involved play the point to completion.

Serve and follow serve to the net (use check stop): Server continues service motion and heads to net, regardless of where the serve goes (good or not). Pause to use the check stop before moving to the ball. Alternate right and left service courts.

Serve or go to net: Service return cannot bounce on server's side. Server moves to the net immediately, closing in so that the return is not allowed to bounce. Utilizing a game situation may increase motivation.

Serve—only one serve per point—and play point: Server is only allowed one service per point. This way, more care is taken toward making the service good.

Volley—two at the net—slow to fast—use point system: Both players stand at the service line. Keep the ball in play between partners. Increase speed of the volley as control can be maintained. Use a point system ("21") to increase motivation and court coverage. Use halfcourt area from side to side (center service line to sideline).

Volley—to baseline rally—try to pass opponent at net: One player at the net, partner at the baseline. Baseliner feeds partner at the net, slowly increasing the tempo until passing shots are used.

Volley—only to forehand or backhand side: Try to pass. Volley goes down the line only. Use the center service line as a guide for the net player and the center mark for the baseliner. Each player goes "down the line" only, but recovers to the line or mark between strokes. Go for winners.

Volley—four at net—keep one ball going: All four begin at the service line and move into the net as able. Each player attempts to keep the volley/half-volley low, causing the opponent to hit up on the shot to clear the net.

Two vs. one at the baseline: One tries to pass two at the net. The two players at the net cover the doubles area, the baseliner covers the singles court only. Attempt to volley the ball so the baseliner must "cover" the baseline area completely. However, discretion is necessary as the net players can easily win the point, thus defeating the purpose of the drill. Change every five minutes. Lobs allowed only at discretion of the coach.

Two vs. one at the net: Two try to pass one at the net. Reverse the drill described in #10 above. Baseliners (two) attempt to pass the volleyer (one). Lobs allowed at discretion of the coach.

Protect your partner—doubles set-up—use rally—attempt to poach: This three-player drill uses a server, receiver and the server's partner. Each player practices each area, including poaching. Rotate every five minutes. Use right and left service courts.

Serve and lob return to backhand quarter of court: This doubles drill is excellent for serving practice and using the lob return of service. Practice the lob over the head of an imaginary net player. Use a bucket of balls for each player.

Return serve to target area on court: Place targets on the court at strategic areas. While the server practices the service, the receiver concentrates on placing the service return to a selected target area.

Serve to target on service court: Place cans, balls, paper targets at critical service areas on the service court, selected to facilitate a weak return or an ace. Practice serving a bucket of balls to these areas.

Depth rally—hit to backcourt area only—use point system: Players remain at the baseline, stroke the ball into the backcourt area between the service line and the baseline. Players may accumulate points by various scoring methods. Games and sets may be played using this drill.

Long rally—count the number of hits between partners: Try for best score—one bounce. Players strive to keep the ball in play without an error. Stroke the ball deep to the backcourt area. No attempt is made to hit winners. This drill is excellent for developing consistency.

Consecutive volleys from inside service line. Count score. Players use a volley rally drill, keeping the ball at moderate speed. Count is maintained to see which team has the longest continuous rally.

Volley rally vs. rebound wall: Number of volleys in one minute. Stand about 12 feet from rebound wall and keep the ball in play using the volley only. Use 30-second to one-minute segments. Can be easily adaptable to competition.

"King of the Court" Singles: Play first to reach 10 points, rotate serve. Winner moves one court toward #1 court, loser stays. Loser on #1 goes to bottom and starts over (singles and doubles).

Use serve and attempt to approach the net: Halfcourt game of 21—lengthwise. All shots must be within half-court area. Put-away smash = 3 points; volley = 2 points; all others = 1 point. Rotate serve each five points. Use serve and attempt to approach the net.

Lob rally: 4 players (2 deep, 2 at net within service line) Net players put away all short lobs. If lob is behind the service court, the net player allows the ball to be played by the baseliner.

Four-ball drill five times: Score by counting the number of balls returned in the singles court. Begin at the baseline. Player is fed a deep shot for rally, short ball for an approach, a volley at the net and a lob for an overhead. Feeder makes no attempt to play the returned balls, but feeds from a basket of balls. Rotate after five trials.

Short game using service courts only: This game utilizes good foot-work and is primarily fun oriented, but it demands ball control. The value in actual game situations is limited.

Figure-eight drill using full court: Two players attempt to keep the ball in play using crosscourt strokes only on one side of the net, and down the line strokes only on the other. This is an aggressive drill demanding skill and stamina. It can be used with one deep and one at the net using the same directions. Attempts are made not to put the ball away, but to extend the partner maximally.

Chapter 14: Evaluation

1. What does the word "progression" mean, and why is it important to the development of skills?

2. Diagram two drills for each of the following shots: forehand, back-hand, volley, lob and service.

3. Explain what is meant by a "dry drill."

4. Three drill areas are basic to good tennis. They are:

Chapter 15

Tournaments and Officiating

Five of the most popular tournaments will be discussed in this chapter: pyramid, ladder, round robin, single elimination and double elimination.

THE PYRAMID TOURNAMENT

The pyramid tournament is used frequently in clubs and camps. It is a tournament that has no ending place, unless time is placed upon the entrants. The pyramid tournament has a large capacity, generally accommodating forty to fifty players.

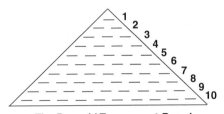

The Pyramid Tournament Board

System of Play
- Each number challenge line "_" is about an inch long (may be longer).
- Place a name on each line in the pyramid, starting at the top.
- The objective of the tournament is to reach the top space, then to defend it against all challengers.
- Players may challenge up one line at a time—best of 3 sets (or pro-sets).
- If the challenged player is defeated, that player changes places with the victor. If the challenged player wins, the position is unchanged.
- The challenged player must respond to the challenge within one week or default. The time is to be arranged by both players involved.
- This tournament allows the challenger to select the style of play best suited to his or her game, thus adding to his chances of success.
- Limit each player to one challenge up every two weeks. Alternate—even lines challenge up one week, odd lines challenge up the next.

THE LADDER TOURNAMENT

Ladder tournaments are fun and excitement is added when time limits are placed on the entrants. The tournament is used frequently by clubs and tennis teams to determine the ranking of players representing the group. Players participate enough times to allow for fair ranking. The best player ends up at the top spot most often, followed by the second best, etc.

Round #1   **Round #2**   **Round #3-**
                                continued

1. _____   1. _____   1. _____
2. _____   2. _____   2. _____
3. _____   3. _____   3. _____
4. _____   4. _____   4. _____
5. _____   5. _____   5. _____
6. _____   6. _____   6. _____
7. _____   7. _____   7. _____
8. _____   8. _____   8. _____
9. _____   9. _____   9. _____
10. _____   10. _____   10. _____

The Ladder Tournament

System of Play

Rank the players as accurately as possible, placing one player on each line of the ladder diagram. Begin in round #1 with the player on line 1 vs. the player on line 2, line 3 vs. line 4, etc. If the number of players is uneven, the bottom player does not have a match this round. In round #1 the even numbers challenge up; in round #2, the odd numbers challenge up (see the diagram above).

A higher-ranked player winning a match keeps the higher position. A lower-ranked player winning changes places with the higher player. When round #2 begins, the top-ranked player does not play, since the player on line two must play down. (Odd numbers challenge up!)

In a ladder tournament:

- Players may challenge only one line up at a time. This is usually arranged by the instructor, coach or tennis pro.
- Ten to 15 rounds should be played, as the ladder changes structure frequently. This many rounds stabilize the ladder.
- This tournament will produce an accurate lineup for future matches or club ranking.

THE ROUND ROBIN TOURNAMENT

Round robin tournaments are used when time is unlimited, as each contestant plays all others. If there are ten players in the tournament, each player must play the other nine entries. This requires many courts and many days. The winner is usually the player who has the highest percentage of wins at the conclusion of the matches. In case of a tie, the two leaders play a match to determine the winner.

A round robin tournament must be scheduled carefully to eliminate confusion. Notice the system below which is used to schedule matches.

Player	A	B	C	D	E	F	G	H	I	J	won	lost	pct.
A	✕												
B		✕											
C			✕										
D				✕									
E					✕								
F						✕							
G							✕						
H								✕					
I									✕				
J										✕			

The round robin tournament

Schedule Procedure: Playing rounds are scheduled below:

#1	#2	#3	#4	#5	#6	#7	#8	#9
A vs. J	A vs. I	A vs. H	A vs. G	A vs. F	A vs. E	A vs. D	A vs. C	A vs. B
B vs. I	J vs. H	I vs. G	H vs. F	G vs. E	F vs. D	E vs. C	D vs. B	C vs. J
C vs. H	B vs. G	J vs. F	I vs. E	H vs. D	G vs. C	F vs. B	E vs. J	D vs. I
D vs. G	C vs. F	B vs. E	J vs. D	I vs. C	H vs. B	G vs. J	F vs. I	E vs. H
E vs. F	D vs. E	C vs. D	B vs. C	J vs. B	I vs. J	H vs. I	G vs. H	F vs. G

(Notice the counterclockwise rotation around team A.)

SINGLE ELIMINATION TOURNAMENTS

Tournament size: A single elimination tournament must be a multiple of two so that it is equal on both top and bottom. A tournament of this type must be either a draw of 4, 8, 16, 32, 64, 128, etc. Most tournaments do not go larger than 32 entries due to time constraints. Probably the most common is a 16 draw (entry). Larger tournaments (district, state or national) may easily be 64 to 128 draw, depending on their importance. For a weekend, a 16 draw is almost ideal.

A tournament may draw men, women, boys, girls, singles, doubles, and mixed doubles. Each of these demands a tournament in itself. Thus, the number of entries in each tournament, the number of courts available, the type of facilities (lighted or not), and the amount of time scheduled, are all important to the success of the event.

Seeding: Seeding is determining who the stronger entries are and separating them to make a better tournament. According to USTA rules, the Tournament Committee determines the seeds, selecting one seed for every four entries, or major portion thereof. For example, if there are thirteen entries, the committee may seed three players. If there are fourteen entries, either three or four may be seeded. The USTA Section governing your area will provide you with specific rules for seeding. They are important and should be followed.

Once the seeded players have been selected, they must be placed in the draw. Generally, in a 16 draw, the first two seeded players will go in the top and bottom spaces on the draw sheet. Who goes where is decided by the flip of a coin or names are drawn out of a hat. The three and four seeds will go at spaces five and 12; follow the same procedure to determine which player goes to each area.

Placing the "byes." A bye is an empty space in the draw sheet. The bye is needed when there are fewer players than are on the draw sheet. For example, if you have 13 entries in your tournament, a 16-entry draw sheet is needed. Since there are not enough players to fill each space, there will be three byes. Byes are placed as outlined in the rules. The word "bye" is placed in the space rather than leaving it blank. The player opposing a bye proceeds to the next round without playing in the first round. All byes are eliminated in the first round.

In placing the byes in the draw, the first bye goes in the open space at the bottom of the draw sheet (space #15), the second bye goes in the first open space in the top (space #2), the third in the bottom (space #13) and the fourth in the top (space #4) and so forth, using this sequence.

The single elimination tournament

Making the draw: Once the seeds and byes have been placed on the draw sheet, the next procedure is to draw the remaining names out of a hat. Names are drawn out one at a time and placed on the draw beginning with the first open space at the top and continuing downward in the order in which they are drawn. If the draw has been made correctly, there are no empty spaces or leftover names.

Assigning the times to play: After completing the draw, assign times for the participants to play and, if possible, assign courts.
Remember:

- Tournament size is a multiple of 2 (4, 8, 16, 32, 64).
- One seed for every four entries.
- Seeds go at 1, 16, 5 and 12, in that order.
- Byes, if needed, begin at 15, then 2, 13, 4, 11, etc., in that order.
- Place times on the sheet to assist players and tournament managers.

DOUBLE ELIMINATION TOURNAMENT

In a double elimination tournament, a player must lose twice before being eliminated. Although this seems to be more favorable for all participants, it is not often used in tournament play. The main reason for this is the lack of time available for tournament play (usually only weekends) and the additional time it takes to play the double elimination bracket.

The tournament is drawn the same as the single elimination tournament, except a loser's bracket is added on the left side of the draw sheet. A player losing on the right (winner's) side moves to the left (loser's) side at approximately the same place in the tournament.

The double elimination tournament meets with the approval of most contestants because a player losing one round is still in the tournament and could eventually win. Double elimination tournaments are best used for small groups of players (eight or less) where time is not a consideration.

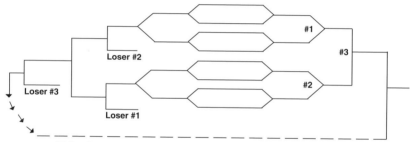

This winner moves over to the winner's side and plays again.

Double elimination tournament

CONSOLATION TOURNAMENTS

There are three consolation tournament draws that have become most popular. They are First Round Consolation, First Match Consolation, and Feed-In Consolation tournaments. When using a First Round Consolation draw, those players who lose in the first round of the main draw are placed in a consolation draw to compete. First Match Consolation draws allow for players who advance in the main draw with the Bye to still be included in the consolation tournament if they are defeated after the first actual match they play. Feed-In Consolations allow for competitors that are defeated in any round of the main draw, up until the semi-finals, to be factored into the consolation tournament. The winner of the Feed-In Consolation is generally considered to finish in 5th place. The winner and finalist of the main draw would finish 1st and 2nd, and the two semi-finalists would play off for 3rd or 4th.

OFFICIATING

The responsibility of officials at tennis events is not easy. Most often officials are a carefully selected group of dedicated men and women who have a deep interest in the sport. They often sacrifice their desire to watch the game from the grandstand to serve in an official position of the court. The official enjoys a position of importance and serves as an instrument of smooth match operation. They sometimes are harassed by spectators or players, and being human, they can make an occasional mistake. However, abuse and mistakes are relatively rare.

There are three officials used in tournament matches. They are the referee, the umpire and the linesman. Each has separate responsibilities, which are described below:

The Referee
- Is appointed by the Tournament Committee.
- Is a member of the committee.
- Makes the draw, assisted by the committee.
- Supervises all aspect of play, including conduct of players, umpires, ball boys, ground crew, etc.
- Appoints a deputy when away from the post.
- Defaults players for reasonable causes.
- Acts as final judge on appeals of defaulted players.
- Schedules matches, assigns courts, suspends play, etc., according to conditions.
- In summation, the referee is in total control of the tournament.

The Umpire (Chair Umpire)
- Conducts the match according to the rules of tennis.
- Assumes the duties of all linesmen not present.
- Asks for the replacement of linesmen, if needed.
- Sees that players on his/her court follow all rules of match play.
- Orders a replay of a point if linesmen are unable to make a call.
- Advises the referee of unfavorable court or match conditions.
- Decides any point of law (rules) concerning the match.
- Defaults a player for cause.

The Linesman (Line Umpire)
- Calls all shots relating to the lines assigned; decisions are **final**.
- Indicates by unsighted signal when unable to make a call.
- Renders a firm opinion on a shot observed in an area outside his or her responsibility only at the chair umpire's request.
- Calls foot faults pertaining to his line, as outlined in the Rules.

The only other official on the court is the net umpire, whose primary responsibility is to call a "let" serve. This person may also keep an additional score card as a backup to the chair umpire.

As an organized sport, a logical chain-of-command is used to assure a smooth, efficiently run athletic event. This is assured by selecting knowledgeable, qualified and experienced personnel to assist the tournament committee in the organization and administration of the tournament. An experienced player should know, recognize and appreciate the responsibilities of all tournament officials. They are, after all, working for the players.

Linesman

Chair umpire

Net umpire

The Tournament Chain-of Command

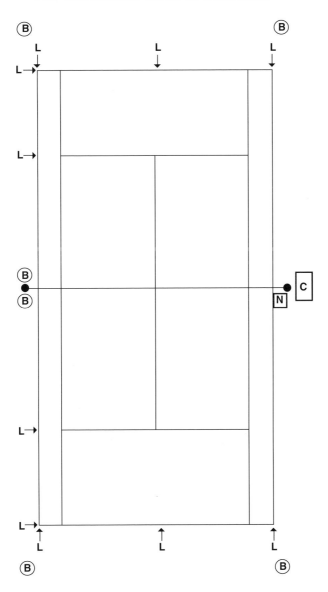

Tournament Committee

(Referee)

C = Chair umpire

N = Net umpire

L = Line umpire

P = Players

B = Ball retrievers

In singles, the linesmen will be positioned on the singles side boundaries instead of the doubles boundaries shown here.

THE USTA POINT PENALTY SYSTEM

The point penalty system (PPS) has been devised by the USTA for three main purposes. They are:

1. to discourage unsportsmanlike conduct,
2. to assure that all players follow the "play must be continuous" rule, and
3. to entice all players to be on time for their scheduled matches.

Some excellent guidelines are given to aid in understanding the PPS. These guidelines are intended to help players, umpires, and officials responsible for conducting tournaments.

Guidelines
1. The Chair Umpire generally issues the point penalty.
2. A flagrantly unsportsmanlike act on the part of a player may result in a default, or a lesser penalty, as a first penalty at the discretion of the Umpire. This may be appealed to the Referee.
3. A player may not appeal to the Referee until the third penalty is given.
4. All penalty points (games) awarded are treated as though those points (games) have actually been played. Changing sides, order of service, new balls are included in this interpretation.
5. A singles player carries into the doubles match all penalties previously assessed, placing this debt onto the doubles team.
6. A player may buy time by using a penalty when suffering from an injury, or due to lack of conditioning.
7. A player must accept the penalty given to the opponent, and continue to play.
8. All penalties given for unsportsmanlike conduct must be reported by the Chair Umpire to the Referee.
9. Subsequent follow-up penalties (suspension, fines, etc.) are not relieved due to point penalties during a tournament.

Violations
- Verbal abuse of another player, or an official.
- Racket abuse, ball abuse, or equipment abuse.
- Improper gestures, profanity, or obscenity, either audible or visible.
- Failure to resume play within three minutes of an injury or after loss of conditioning.
- Intentional delay of the game at any time.

Penalties
First Offense	Warning
Second Offense	Point Penalty
Third Offense	Game Penalty
Fourth Offense	Default of Match

Lateness Penalties
Up to 5 minutes	Loss of Toss + 1 game
5 to 10 minutes	Loss of Toss + 2 games
10 to 15 minutes	Loss of Toss + 3 games
Over 15 minutes	Default

Chapter 15: Evaluation

1. Why is the ladder tournament used by most tennis coaches?

2. List advantages and disadvantages for the following tournaments: ladder, round robin, single elimination and double elimination.

3. Why are players sometimes seeded?

4. Where do you place byes on a draw sheet?

5. Which tournament allows you to lose twice before being eliminated?

6. What is the difference between a tennis umpire and a tennis referee?

7. Why are byes sometimes necessary for tournaments?

Appendixes

Contents

APPENDIX A: RESOURCES

References

Books and Articles

Ashe, Arthur, with Frank Deford. *Arthur Ashe: Portrait in Motion.* Boston: Haughton Mifflin Co.

Barnaby, John. *Advantage Tennis.* Boston: Allyn and Bacon, Inc.

Barnaby, John M. *Advantage Tennis: Racket Work, Tactics, and Logic.* Boston: Allyn and Bacon, Inc.

Brown, Jim. *Tennis: Teaching, Coaching, and Directing Programs.* Englewood Cliffs, NJ: Prentice-Hall, Inc.

Brown, Jim. *Tennis Without Lessons.* Englewood Cliffs, NJ: Prentice-Hall, Inc.

Gallwey, W. Timothy. *The Inner Game of Tennis.* NY: Random House.

Gensemer, R.E. *Tennis.* Saunders and Co.

Gould, Dick. *Tennis Anyone?* Palo Alto, CA: Mayfield Publishing Company.

Harman, Bob and Keith Monroe. *Use Your Head in Tennis.* NY: Crowell.

Johnson, Joan D. and Paul J. Xanthos. *Tennis.* Dubuque, Iowa: William C. Brown Co.

King, Billie Jean and Kim Chapin. *Tennis to Win.* NY: Harper and Row.

Mason, R. Elaine. *Tennis.* Boston: Allyn and Bacon, Inc.

McPhee, John. *Wimbledon: A Celebration.* NY: The Viking Press.

Murphy, Bill. *Complete Book of Championship Tennis Drills.* West Nyack, NY: Parker Publishing Co., Inc.

Murphy, Chet. *Advanced Tennis.* Dubuque, Iowa: Wm. C. Brown, Co.

Murphy, Chet and Bill Murphy. *Tennis for the Player, Teacher and Coach.* Philadelphia: W.B. Saunders Co.

Newcombe, John and Angie with Clarence Mabry. *The Family Tennis Book. Tennis* magazine with Quadrangle. The New York Times Book Co.

Powell, Nick. *The Code.* Princeton, NJ: United States Lawn Tennis Association.

Ramo, Simon. *Extraordinary Tennis for the Ordinary Player.* NY: Crown Publishers, Inc.

Talbert, Bill with Gordon Greer. *Weekend Tennis.* Garden City, NY: Doubleday and Co., Inc.

Talbert, William and Editors of *Sports Illustrated. The Sports Illustrated Book of Tennis.* Philadelphia: J.B. Lippincott Co.

Tilmanis, Gundars A. *Advanced Tennis for Coaches, Teachers and Players.* Philadelphia: Lea and Febiger.

United States Lawn Tennis Assoc. *Official Encyclopedia of Tennis.* NY: Harper and Row.

United States Tennis Assoc. *USTA Official Yearbook.* 51 E., 42nd St., NY, 10017.

Magazines and other Periodicals

ADDvantage, trade magazine for men and women teaching professionals, USPTA Inc., One USPTA Centre, 3535 Briarpark Dr., Houston, TX 77042. (713) 978-7782, FAX (713) 978-7780.

The Art of Tennis. Greg Schwartz.

Tennis. Monthly. New York Times Sports and Leisure Magazines, 5520 Park Ave., Box 395, Trumbull, Conn. 06611-0395. (203) 373-7000.

Tennis Illustrated. Monthly. Devonshire Publication Co., 630 Shatto Place, Los Angeles, CA 90005.

Tennis Industry. Bi-monthly. 79 Madison Avenue, 8th Floor, New York 10016, (212) 921-3784, FAX: (212) 921-3777.

Tennis, The Magazine of the Racquet Sports. Official monthly publication of the USPTA. Tennis Features, Inc., 297 Westport Ave., Norwalk, CT 06856.

Tennis Magazine. Monthly. USTA, 70 West Red Oak Lane, White Plains, NY 10604.

The Tennis Players Handbook. Tennis Magazine Editors, Simon & Schuster.

Tennis Week. Tennis News Inc., 124 East 40th St., Suite 1101, New York 10016. (212) 808-4750.

Tennis World. Royal London House, 171B High St., Beckenham, Kent, BR31BY, England.

Winning Tennis: Strokes and Strategies of the Top Pros. Stockton, Dick and Wendy Overton, The Chilton Co.

World Tennis Magazine. Box 3, Grace Station, NY 10028.

Note:

There are literally hundred's of tennis books on the market today. It is most difficult to recommend one above the other without a full review. In order to view a good distribution of material, use your computer and click on to www.amazon.com or a similar web site, then type in "Tennis Books". The current listing is over 200. We are delighted this text is one of those.

Selected Video List

Championship Tennis, Morris Video Sports Series #219. Morris Video, Box 443, Redondo Beach, CA 90277.

How to Play Winning Doubles—And Stay the Best of Friends!, Vic Braden. Tennis Magazine Home Video, Golf Digest/Tennis Inc., 1986. Tennis Video's USA, 675 E. Big Beaver Rd., Suite 209, Troy, MI 48083.

Mental Toughness, Tips for Better Tennis, Jim Loehr. Peak Performance, Inc., Box 2829, Duxbury, MA 02332.

Over 150 Winning Tennis Tips, BNW Productions. Sports Direct, USA, 675 E. Big Beaver Rd., Suite 209, Troy, MI 48083.

Smash Hit, American Twist Productions. American Twist, 650 N. Bronson, Los Angeles, CA 90004.

Tennis for the Future, Vic Braden. Volume I and II. Paramount Home Video, 5555 Melrose Ave., Hollywood, CA 90038.

Tennis Talk, Dennis Van Der Meer. Sports Direct, USA, 675 E. Big Beaver Rd., Suite 209, Troy, MI 48083.

Vic Braden's Quick Cures for Common Tennis Problems, Tennis Magazine. Sports Direct, USA, 675 E. Big Beaver Rd., Suite 209, Troy, MI 48083.

As with tennis books of various types, tennis videos are many and of different subject areas. The author has perused this field and found hundreds of types of videos available to the tennis and racket sports enthusiast. Again, as with tennis books, the scope and content are too numerous to mention. However, one may either use a computer or similar source to see what is offered. Here are some suggestions:

www.thetennischannel.com - hundreds of films available

Other films and videos may be found at the following sites:

www.shopzilla.com
www.activevideos.com
www.sportsnationvideos.com
www.bizrate.com
www.tennislifemagazine.com
www.dealtime.com

NATIONAL AND SECTIONAL OFFICES
OF THE UNITED STATES TENNIS ASSOCIATION

National Offices:

United States Tennis Association Inc., 70 West Red Oak Lane, White Plains, NY 10604, (919) 696-7000.

United States Tennis Association Editorial and Production Offices, 5520 Park Ave., Box 395, Trumbull, CT 06611-0395. (203) 373-7000.

Sectional Offices:

Caribbean Tennis Assoc., PO Box 40439, San Juan, PR 00940-0439. (787) 726-8782, FAX: (787) 982-7783.

Eastern Tennis Assoc., 550 Mamaroneck Ave., Suite 209, Harrison, NY 10528; (914) 698-0414, FAX: (914) 698-2471.

Florida Tennis Assoc., 1 Deuce Court, Suite 100, Daytona Beach, FL 32124; (386) 671-8949, FAX: (386) 671-8948.

Hawaii Pacific Tennis Assoc., 1500 South Beretania St., Suite 300, Honolulu, HI 96826. (808) 955-6696, FAX: (808) 955-8363.

Intermountain Tennis Assoc., 1201 South Parker Rd., Suite 200, Denver, CO 80231. (303) 695-4117, FAX: (303) 695-6518.

Mid-Atlantic Tennis Assoc., 7926 Jones Branch Drive, Suite 120, McLean, VA 22101. (703) 556-6120, FAX: (703) 556-6175.

Middle States Tennis Association, 1288 Valley Forge Rd., Suite 73, P.O. Box 987, Valley Forge, PA 19482-0987. (610) 935-5000, FAX: (610) 935-5484

Midwest Tennis Association, 8720 Castle Creek Parkway, Suite 329, Indianapolis, IN 46205. (317) 577-5130, FAX: (317) 577-5131.

Missouri Valley Tennis Assoc., 8676 West 96th St., Suite 100, Overland Park, KS 66212. (913) 322-4800, FAX: (913) 322-4801.

New England Tennis Association, 110 Turnpike Road, Westborough, MA 01581. (508) 366-3450, FAX: (508) 366-5805.

Northern California Tennis Association, 1350 Loop Rd., Suite 100, Alameda, CA 94502-7081. (510) 748-7373, FAX: (510) 748-7377.

Northern Tennis Association, 1001 West 98th Street, Suite 101, Bloomington, MN 55431. (952) 887-5061.

Pacific Northwest Tennis Association, 4840 SW Western Ave., Suite 300, Beaverton, OR 97005-3430. (503) 520-1877, FAX: (503) 520-0133.

Southern California Tennis Association, P.O. Box 240015, Los Angeles, CA 90024-9115. (310) 208-3838, FAX: (310) 824-7691.

Southern Tennis Association, 5686 Spalding Drive, Norcross, GA 30092-2504. (770) 368-8200, FAX: (770) 368-9091.

Southwestern Tennis Association, 2720 E. Thomas Rd., Suite B120, Phoenix, AZ 85016. (602) 956-6855.

Texas Tennis Association, 8105 Exchange, Austin, TX 78754. (512) 443-1334, FAX: (512) 443-4748.

Other Supporting Agencies:

United States Professional Tennis Association Inc., One USPTA Centre, 3535 Briarpark Dr., Houston, TX 77042. (713) 978-7782, FAX: (713) 978-7780.

United States Tennis Association Membership Services Center, 121 South Service Rd., Jerico, NY 11753, (516) 333-7990.

APPENDIX B: NATIONAL TENNIS RATING PROGRAM

Several years ago, the National Tennis Association (NTA), in cooperation with the United States Tennis Association (USTA) and the United States Professional Tennis Association (USPTA), undertook a study of the tennis rating systems that were proliferating at the time. There were a dozen such rating systems in addition to the traditional methods of classification. With the rapid increase in the number of tennis players regularly participating in programs, a universal rating program was necessary.

To be successful, a rating program had to be universally accepted, free, easy to administer and non-exclusive. With this in mind, the NTA, USTA, USPTA and the IRSA chose to adopt and promote the National Tennis Rating Program (NTRP) to unify the method of classifying players throughout the country. The sponsoring organizations believe that the NTRP is a simple, self-placement method for grouping individuals of similar ability levels and that it allows players to achieve better competition, on-court compatibility, personal challenge and more enjoyment in the sport.

Self-rating Guidelines

The National Tennis Rating Program provides a simple, initial self-placement method of grouping individuals of similar ability levels for league play, tournaments, group lessons, social competition and club or community programs.

The rating categories are generalizations about skill levels. You may find that you actually play above or below the category that best describes your skill level, depending on your competitive ability. The category you choose is not meant to be permanent, but may be adjusted as your skills change or as your match play demonstrates the need for reclassification. Ultimately your rating is based upon your results in match play.

To place yourself:
A. Begin with 1.0. Read all categories carefully and then decide which one best describes your present ability level.
B. Be certain that you qualify on all points of all preceding categories as well as those in the classification you choose.
C. When rating yourself, assume you are playing against a player of the same sex and the same ability.
D. Your self-rating may be verified by a teaching professional, coach, league coordinator or other qualified expert.
E. The person in charge of your tennis program has the right to reclassify you if your self-placement is thought to be inappropriate based on match results.

NTRP Rating Categories

1.0 This player is just starting to play tennis.

1.5 This player has limited playing experience and is still working primarily on getting the ball over the net; has some knowledge of scoring but is not familiar with basic positions and procedures for singles and doubles play.

2.0 This player may have had some lessons, but needs on-court experience; has obvious stroke weaknesses but is beginning to feel comfortable with singles and doubles play.

2.5 This player has more dependable strokes and is learning to judge where the ball is going; has weak court coverage or is often caught out of position, but is starting to keep the ball in play with other players of the same ability.

3.0 This player can place shots with moderate success; can sustain a rally of slow pace but is not comfortable with all strokes; lacks control when trying for power.

3.5 This player has achieved stroke dependability and direction on shots within reach, including forehand, backhand volleys, but still lacks depth and variety; seldom double faults and occasionally forces errors on the serve.

4.0 This player has dependable strokes on both forehand and backhand sides; has the ability to use a variety of shots including lobs, overheads, approach shots and volleys; can place the first serve and force some errors; is seldom out of position in a doubles game.

4.5 This player has begun to master the use of power and spin; has sound footwork; can control depth of shots and is able to move opponent up and back; can hit first serves with power and accuracy and place the second serve; is able to rush net with some success on serve in singles as well as doubles.

5.0 This player has good shot anticipation; frequently has an outstanding shot or exceptional consistency around which a game may be structured; can regularly hit winners or force errors off of short balls; can successfully execute lobs, drop shots, half volleys and overhead smashes; has good depth and spin on most second serves.

5.5 This player can execute all strokes offensively and defensively, can hit dependable shots under pressure, is able to analyze opponents styles and can employ patterns of play to assure the greatest possibility of winning the point. This player can hit winners or force errors with both first and second serves, and return of service can be an effective weapon.

6.0 This player has mastered all of the above skills, has developed power and/or consistency as a major weapon and can vary strategies and styles of play in a competitive situation. This player typically has had intensive training for national competition at junior or college levels.

6.5 This player has mastered all of the above skills and is an experienced tournament competitor who regularly travels for competition and whose income may be partially derived from prize winnings.

7.0 This is a world class player.

Rating Categories

1.0-1.9	Beginner	4.0-4.9	Advanced
2.0-2.9	Advanced beginner	5.0 and up	Tournament and/or ranked
3.0-3.9	Intermediate		

Name _____ Rating _____

Instructor's Comments: _____

_____

_____

_____

Instructor's rating _____

Instructor's signature _____

APPENDIX C: TENNIS SCORE CARD

Directions for Completing Tennis Score Card
(Card is located on the back of these directions)

1. Fill in information concerning players, event, date, name and school in the space provided.

2. Place the initial of the server (singles or doubles) in the space indicated on the score card under SI (server's initials)

3. Place the player's initials on the right side of the card in the space provided in order to keep an accurate tally of the games won.

4. The check under the column CB is provided as a reminder to change balls if you are using the 9-11 ball change sequence.

5. When scoring points on the card, use a slash " / " diagonally across the small square to indicate which player won.

6. Use the top line always for the server's score in the game being played.

7. At the conclusion of the game, mark the "game" column appropriately for the player winning the game just concluded. Use "1" then "2" etc., until the set is completed.

8. If a tie-breaker is used when the score is six-all, the bottom of the chart is used, where the "TB" (tie-breaker) is located (below 17). The markings indicate where the service is made (right or left), and the letters R and L in the upper and lower squares indicate that the players are serving from opposite sides of the net. The double line indicates that the players change sides of the court before serving the next point.

9. At the end of the tiebreaker, the score of 7 is written into the winner's column. The opponent's score is ended with 6. Thus the final score of the set is 7-6.

10. When scoring a match, you would be given sufficient scorecards to continue through three sets, if the match lasts that long.

Tennis Score Card

Event _____ Date _____

Player _____
       Name   *School*

Player _____
       Name   *School*

Winner _____ Umpire _____

(At conclusion of match, the umpire must sign this score card and take immediately to official.)

CB		SI	Players change sides after 1st game, 3rd game, etc. POINTS - SET NO. 1																	Player Initials Game
	1																			
	2																			
	3																			
	4																			
	5																			
	6																			
	7																			
	8																			
√	9																			
	10																			
	11																			
	12																			
	13																			
	14																			
	15																			
	16																			
	17																			
TB			R		L	R			L	R			L	R			L		
				L	R			L	R			L	R			L	R		

CB= Change balls; SI= Server's Initials; TB= Tie-breaker; L= Left; R = Right.

Set No. 1   Won by _____ Score _____

Name _____

APPENDIX D: ERROR CHART
First Set

Game # Server	1st Serve Fault	Serve Returns				Groundstrokes				Volleys		Winners		Aces	Smash		Dbl Flt	Game
		FHN	FHO	BHN	BHO	FHN	FHO	BHN	BHO	NET	OUT	US	OPP		NET	OUT	US OPP	Won by
1																			
2																			
3																			
4																			
5																			
6																			
7																			
8																			
9																			
10																			
11																			
12																			
TB																			

KEY: **FHN** = FOREHAND INTO NET, **FHO** = FOREHAND OUT. **BHN** = BACKHAND INTO NET. BHO = BACKHAND OUT
Use a "✔" to indicate your mark in the appropriate column.

APPENDIX E: TENNIS EXAMINATION

True/False: Circle T for true statements or F for false statements

T F 1. A competition between the U.S. and England for women only, is called the Wightman Cup Championships.

T F 2. A half-volley is a stroke whereby the racket contacts the ball just as it rebounds from the court and very near the ground.

T F 3. As a general rule, most tennis players do not warm up properly.

T F 4. A score of deuce indicates that both players have won at least four points each, and both have the same score.

T F 5. As the server, I have won two points to my opponent's three. The score in this game is 40-30.

T F 6. A chop shot places severe topspin on the tennis ball.

T F 7. A right hander who consistently hits the ball to the right is probably swinging late.

T F 8. Put-away overhead smashes should not be attempted from behind the baseline.

T F 9. Most approach shots should be hit down the line

T F 10. Drop shots should not be attempted when the wind is in the hitter's face.

T F 11. The volley is an offensive weapon.

T F 12. The tennis grip should be loosened or relaxed between shots.

T F 13. Player A is slightly outside the court when hit by player B's over-head smash. Since the ball did not touch the ground before hitting player A, the point should be awarded to player B.

T F 14. If you are right handed, a wide slice serve from the deuce court is an effective serve to a left hander.

T F 15. The service toss that is thrown too far out front will usually cause the ball to be hit long.

T F 16. The hardest serve to master is the cannonball, or flat serve.

T F 17. In good doubles play, most serves should go to the opponent's backhand side.

T F 18. If there is one point in a game that is more important than others, it is probably the fourth point when the score is 30-15 or 15-30.

T F 19. A shot is good if it is returned outside the net post and lands in the proper court.

T   F   20. Follow through will increase the depth of a volley.

T   F   21. A pusher or retriever is not usually a strong net player.

T   F   22. An Eastern grip increases ball spin on service.

T   F   23. The server must have at least one foot in contact with the ground when the ball is stroked.

T   F   24. Participants are technically allowed three minutes when changing ends of the court between games.

T   F   25. If a receiver claims to be not ready and does not make an effort to return a serve, the server may not claim the point even though the service was good.

T   F   26. A good axiom to follow is "play every point" and give nothing away.

T   F   27. It is illegal to serve underhand in tennis.

T   F   28. A player's request for the removal of a ball must be honored at any time.

T   F   29. Under no circumstances may you reach over the net to strike the ball.

T   F   30. A player standing outside the court volleys a ball into the opponent's court. The rally should continue.

T   F   31. If my serve hits my doubles partner before striking the court, a let serve is declared.

T   F   32. Any shot that hits a loose ball within the court is automatically declared a replay.

T   F   33. A server's partner may not take a position that blocks the view of the receiver.

T   F   34. Team A loses a lob in the sun and wind and it drops, hitting one of their players on top of the head, however, the partner makes a winning shot off of the first bounce. Point should be awarded to Team A.

T   F   35. It is a fault if the ball is missed in attempting the service.

T   F   36. An Eastern grip will impart less speed of service than a Continental grip.

T   F   37. When returning serve from a left hander and the ball has spin, it is safe to assume that the ball will move to your right depending upon the severity of the spin.

T   F   38. A right handed hitter who consistently pulls the ball to their left is probably hitting too soon.

T   F   39. In doubles, the server of the third game will also serve the fifth game.

T   F   40. Before coming to the net you should wait for a ball that lands short.

T   F   41. The best volleying grip for the single handed hitter is the Eastern grip.

T   F   42.   When you bisect the angle of return you place yourself on a line from your opponent which allows you the most court coverage for your forehand.

T   F   43.   The difference in width between the doubles and singles tennis court is eight feet.

T   F   44.   Good doubles strategy generally has the weakest server serving first.

T   F   45.   If you are clearly outclassed, it is good strategy to go to a reckless chance taking type of play.

T   F   46.   If you are losing a match it is good strategy to slow the play to try and get yourself together.

T   F   47.   Players always change court ends at the conclusion of each set.

T   F   48.   It is considered poor sportsmanship to stroke a shot directly at your opponent.

T   F   49.   Player A charges to the net to return a drop shot. He returns the ball for a winner, but to keep from touching the net, he jumps over it while the ball is in play. A should receive the point as long as he did not interfere with his opponent's shot.

T   F   50.   In match play, play may be temporarily suspended because of fatigue to a player.

T   F   51.   You should poach whenever your serving partner is weak or struggling.

T   F   52.   Move your doubles team as a gate, i.e., up and back together.

T   F   53.   It is absolutely imperative that you place the ball in play each time your opponent serves to you.

T   F   54.   Should you miss a serve (you are serving) it is better to miss short than long.

T   F   55.   When playing competitively, never volley or smash to the deep opponent, always the closest one.

T   F   56.   When poaching, chop shots are not good balls to chase.

T   F   57.   When your partner is on the baseline and you are poaching, never cross the center line of the court and then attempt to scurry back.

T   F   58.   More spin on your serve allows more time to take the net.

T   F   59.   In doubles, if you are pulled wide, your partner must close the center gap and give more alley to the opponents.

T   F   60.   Keeping your shots deep is not as important in doubles as in singles.

T   F   61.   It is not good strategy to attempt a volley on a dead run.

T   F   62.   Never stay on that side of the court if the ball goes over your head and your partner is on the baseline.

T F   63. You should poach whenever it makes your opponent nervous.

T F   64. It is good strategy to aggressively poach if your team is having trouble winning on a particular side of the court.

T F   65. It is easier to lengthen a short serve than to shorten a long serve.

T F   66. In general, do not attempt to return a serve in singles with a lob shot.

T F   67. If a served ball brushes the server's partner's shirt, but does not actually hit him, it is a fault.

Multiple Choice: Choose the appropriate answer for each question. Use only one best answer for each question.

_____ 68. What is the difference in width between the doubles and the singles court in tennis?
    a. 7 feet
    b. 8 feet
    c. 9 feet
    d. 10 feet

_____ 69. In playing a set, the most crucial game is
    a. third
    b. fifth
    c. sixth
    d. seventh

_____ 70. In the 12 point tiebreaker, the fifth point is served to the
    a. even service court
    b. odd service court
    c. neither court

_____ 71. In doubles, the server of the third game will also serve the
    a. fifth game
    b. sixth game
    c. seventh game
    d. eighth game

_____ 72. The best volleying grip is the
    a. Western
    b. Eastern
    c. Shake hands grip
    d. Continental

_____ 73. Which of the following will have the greatest speed if other things are equal.
    a. topspin
    b. backspin
    c. no spin
    d. sidespin

_____ 74. When may a doubles team change its order of serving?
    a. at the beginning of the game in a set
    b. at any time during the match
    c. at the beginning of any set
    d. the serving order may not be changed during a match

75. Which of the following would be a completed match?
    a. 6-4, 3-6   c. 6-2, 0-6, 7-5
    b. 7-5, 8-7, 6-0   d. 6-3, 6-4, 5-7

76. The game of tennis was introduced in the U.S. by
    a. Fred Perry
    b. Helen Wightman
    c. Clarence Davis
    d. Mary Outerbridge

77. If a ball rolls onto the court during a rally, the point
    a. should be continued
    b. is awarded to the player on whose side the ball is rolling
    c. should be replayed
    d. the umpire may rule for either player

78. The third point is yours, the score is now
    a. love-40
    b. 15-30
    c. advantage server
    d. 30-15

79. Your opponent, after a long rally, wins the next point with an overhead. The score is now
    a. deuce
    b. advantage server
    c. advantage receiver
    d. 30-30

80. A defensive lob is different from an offensive lob due to
    a. control
    b. height and spin
    c. spin and depth
    d. speed and placement

81. In doubles, your best strategy for winning the point outright against two opponents at the net would be to
    a. lob over their heads
    b. hit softly at their feet
    c. drive directly at one or the other
    d. drive between them

82. During play, but after the serve, the server swings at a ball but misses it. The ball lands outside the baseline. What is the ruling?
    a. point for the receiving side
    b. a let is played
    c. point for the serving side
    d. the ball remains in play

83. In doubles, on the second serve, the served ball hits the net cord and then drops into the receiver's alley. The receiver cannot reach the ball in time to return it. What is the correct ruling?
    a. the serve is a let
    b. the serve is a fault
    c. the server wins the point
    d. the server loses the point

Completion

84. A _____ _____ is a softly hit ball having backspin which barely clears the net.

85. To win a game served by your opponent is to _____ service.

86. When a net player cuts off a return shot from an opponent it is called _____.

87. Never follow a _____ shot to the net.

88. Never lob to the _____overhead.

89. Never volley or kill to the _____opponent.

90. Ground strokes are _____ important in doubles than singles.

91. In doubles, the best way to keep a poacher anchored in one spot, is to frequently hit the ball _____ _____.

92. The most important points are most often played in the _____ _____.

93. _____ _____ are probably the most important part of a tennis players wardrobe.

94. Tennis courts should be laid out on a _____ _____ line.

95. The standard dimension of a tennis court is _____ x _____.

96. The saying, "If I can somehow hit one more shot back than you, I will win the point," is an expression of the _____theory.

97. When coming to the net to volley a shot, you should _____ before volleying the ball.

98. Good doubles is based upon the server being able to _____ _____.

99. _____ is a method of determining who the better players or teams are, and separating them to make for a better tournament.

100. Topsin causes the tennis ball to _____ quickly after clearing the net.

APPENDIX F: 2006 RULES OF TENNIS

1. THE COURT (OLD 1 & 34)

The court shall be a rectangle, 78 feet (23.77m) long and, for singles matches, 27 feet (8.23 m) wide. For doubles matches, the court shall be 36 feet (10.97m) wide.

The court shall be divided across the middle by a net suspended by a cord or metal cable which shall pass over or be attached to two net posts at a height of 3 1/2 feet (1.07m). The net shall be fully extended so that it completely fills the space between the two net posts and it must be of sufficiently small mesh to ensure that a ball cannot pass through it. The height of the net shall be 3 feet (0.914m) at the centre, where it shall be held down tightly by a strap. A band shall cover the cord or metal cable and the top of the net. The strap and band shall be completely white.

- The maximum diameter of the cord or metal cable shall be 1/3 inch (0.8cm).
- The maximum width of the strap shall be 2 inches (5cm).
- The band shall be between 2 inches (5cm) and 2 1/2 inches (6.35cm) deep on each side.

For doubles matches, the centres of the net posts shall be 3 feet (0.914 m) outside the doubles court on each side.

For singles matches, if a singles net is used, the centres of the posts shall be 3 feet (0.914m) outside the singles court on each side. If a doubles net is used, then the net shall be supported, at a height of 3 1/2 feet (1.07m), by two singles sticks, the centres of which shall be 3 feet (0.914m) outside the singles court on each side.

- The net post shall not be more than 6 inches (15cm) square or 6 inches (15 cm) square or 6 inches (15cm) in diameter.
- The singles sticks shall not be more than 3 inches (7.5 cm) square or 3 inches (7.5 cm) square or 3 inches (7.5 cm) in diameter.
- The net posts and singles sticks shall not be more than 1 inch (2.5 cm) above the top of the net cord.

The lines at the ends of the court are called baselines and the lines at the sides of the court are called sidelines.

Two lines shall be drawn between the singles sidelines, 21 feet (6.40 m) from each side of the net, parallel with the net. These lines are called the servicelines. On each side of the net, the area between the serviceline and the net shall be divided into two equal parts, the service courts, by the centre serviceline. The centre serviceline shall be drawn parallel with the singles sidelines and half way between them.

Each baseline shall be divided in half by a centre mark, 4 inches (10 cm) in length, which shall be drawn inside the court and parallel with the singles sidelines.

- The centre service line and centre mark shall be 2 inches (5 cm) wide.
- The other lines of the court shall be between 1 inch (2.5 cm) and 2 inches (5 cm) wide, except that the base lines may be up to 4 inches (10 cm) wide.

All court measurements shall be made to the outside of the lines and all lines of the court shall be of the same colour clearly contrasting with the colour of the surface.

No advertising is allowed on the court, net, strap, band, net posts or singles sticks except as provided in **Appendix III**.

USTA Comment 1.1: *How do you tighten the net to the proper tension?* First, loosen the center strap. Next, tighten the net cord until the center of the net is approximately 40 inches above the ground. Finally, tighten the center strap until the center of the net is 36 inches above the ground. These measurements should always be made before the day's first match and when possible before each match.

USTA Comment 1.2: *What happens if a singles stick falls to the court during a point?* The point stops immediately and is replayed.

2. PERMANENT FIXTURES (OLD 2)

The permanent fixtures of the court include the backstops and sidestops, the spectators, the stands and seats for spectators, all other fixtures around and above the court, the chair umpire, line umpires, net umpire and ball persons when in their recognized positions.

In a singles match played with a doubles net and singles sticks, the net posts and the part of the net outside the singles sticks are permanent fixtures and are not considered as net posts or part of the net.

3. THE BALL (OLD 3, 13, 27, & 32)

Balls, which are approved for play under the Rules of Tennis, must comply with the specifications in **Appendix I**.

The International Tennis Federation shall rule on the question of whether any ball or prototype complies with Appendix I or is otherwise approved, or not approved, for play. Such ruling may be taken on its own initiative, or upon application by any party with a bona fide interest therein, including any player, equipment manufacturer or National Association or members thereof. Such rulings and applications shall be made in accordance with the applicable Review and Hearing Procedures of the International Tennis Federation (see **Appendix VI**).

The event organizers must announce in advance of the event:

a. The number of balls for play (2, 3, 4 or 6).

b. The ball change policy, if any.

Ball changes, if any, can be made either:

    i. After an agreed odd number of games, in which case, the first ball change in the match shall take place two games earlier than for the rest of the match, to make allowance for the warm-up. A tie-break game counts as one game for the ball change. A ball change shall not take place at the beginning of a tie-break game. In this case, the ball change shall be delayed until the beginning of the second game of the next set; or

    ii. At the battening of a set.

If a ball gets broken during play, the point shall be replayed.

Case 1: If a ball is soft at the end of a point, should the point be replayed?

Decision: If the ball is soft, not broken, the point shall not be replayed.

Note: Any ball to be used in a tournament which is played under the Rules of Tennis, must be named on the official ITF list of approved balls issued by the International Tennis Federation.

> **USTA Comment 3.1:** *What is the difference between a broken ball and a soft ball?* A broken ball has no compression; a soft ball has some compression. Both broken and soft balls should be removed from play.
>
> **USTA Comment 3.2:** *May a player cause a ball to become wet by using the ball to wipe perspiration from the player's body?* No. A player may not take any action that materially changes the condition of the ball; therefore, a player may not use a ball to wipe off perspiration.
>
> **USTA 3.3:** *A current list of USTA approved balls is available on the USTA web site, www.usta.com.*

4. THE RACKET (OLD 4)

Rackets, which are approved for play under the Rules of Tennis, must comply with the specifications in **Appendix II**.

The International Tennis Federation shall rule on the question of whether any racket or prototype complies with **Appendix II** or is otherwise approved, or not approved, for play. Such ruling may be undertaken on its own initiative, or upon application by any party with a bona fide interest therein, including any player, equipment manufacturer or National Association or members thereof. Such rulings and applications shall be made in accordance with the applicable Review and Hearing Procedures of the International Tennis Federation (see **Appendix VI**).

Case 1: Is more than one set of strings allowed on the hitting surface of a racket?

Decision: No. The rule mentions a pattern (not patterns) of crossed strings. (See **Appendix II**)

Case 2: Is the stringing pattern of a racket considered to be generally uniform and flat if the strings are on more than one plane?

Decision: No

Case 3: Can vibration dampening devices be placed on the strings of a racket? If so, where can they be placed?

Decision: Yes, but these devices may only be placed outside the pattern of the crossed strings.

Case 4: During a point, a player accidentally breaks a string. Can the player continue to play another point with this racket?

Decision: Yes, except where specifically prohibited by event organizers.

Case 5: Is a player allowed to use more than one racket at any time during play?

Decision: No.

Case 6: Can a battery that affects playing characteristics be incorporated into a racket?

Decision: No. A battery is prohibited because it is an energy source, as are solar cells and other similar devices.

> **USTA Comment 4.1:** *What happens if it is discovered after play has begun that a player has been using an illegal racket or an illegally strung racket?* All points played stand. The player must find another racket before continuing a play. A player is subject to code violations for delay under the Point Penalty System. If the discovery occurs after the match is over, the match still counts.
>
> **USTA Comment 4.2:** *May a player who breaks a racket or a string in a racket leave the court to get a replacement?* A player who leaves the Court to get a replacement is subject to Code Violations for delays under the Point Penalty System. Rule 29b permits a player "reasonable extra time" to leave the court only in those cases where "clothing, footwear or necessary equipment (excluding racket) is broken or needs to be replaced."

5. SCORE IN A GAME (OLD 26 & 27)

a. Standard game

A standard game is scored as follows with the server's score being called first:

No point	-	"Love"
First point	-	"15"
Second point	-	"30"
Third point	-	"40"
Fourth point	-	"Game"

except that if each player/team has won three points, the score is "Deuce". After "Deuce", the score is "Advantage" for the player/team who wins the next point. If that same player/team also wins the next point, that player/team wins the "Game"; if the opposing player/team wins the next point, the score is again "Deuce". A player/team needs to win two consecutive points immediately after "Deuce" to win the "Game".

b. Tie-break game

During a tie-break game, points are scored "Zero", "1", "2", "3", etc. The first player/team to win seven points wins the "Game" and "Set", provided there is a margin of two points over the opponent(s). If necessary, the tie-break game shall continue until this margin is achieved.

The player whose turn it is to serve shall serve the first point of the tie-break game. The following two points shall be served by the opponent(s) (in doubles, the player of the opposing team due to serve next). After this, each player/team shall serve alternately for two consecutive points until the end of the tie-break game (in doubles, the rotation of service within each team shall continue in the same order as during that set).

The player/team whose turn it was to serve first in the tie-break game shall the receiver in the first game of the following set.

Additional approved alternative scoring methods can be found in **Appendix IV**.

USTA Comment 5.1: Numeric scoring, which consists of "zero," "one," "two," and "three," may be substituted for "Love," "15," "30," and "40" as long as the principle of winning four points by a margin of two is preserved. This is particularly appropriate for matches between new or young players or in which one player does not understand English. Hand signals may be used to show the score. This is a common practice with players who are hearing impaired.

USTA Comment 5.2: The tiebreak game should not be confused with the Match Tiebreak (7-point or 10-point), which under certain circumstances may be played in lieu of the deciding final set. The Match Tiebreak is described in **Appendix IV**.

USTA Comment 5.3: Is the server required to call the score at the beginning of each game and the point scores as the games go on in matches without officials? Yes. This is required by *The Code § 31*. After an official has cautioned a player to call out the score, the official may in a particularly egregious case treat subsequent violations as Code Violations for unsportsmanlike conduct.

USTA Comment 5.4: *The server states that the score is 40-15; the receiver states that the score is 30-30. The players agree on who won every point except for the second point. What should they do?* They should replay the second point from the advantage court. If the server wins the point, the score becomes 40-15; if the receiver wins the point, the score becomes 30-30. The next point is played from the deuce court.

USTA Comment 5.5: *What happens in the same situation as **USTA Comment 5.4** except that the disputed point is the third point?* Everything is done the same except that the disputed point is played from the deuce court.

USTA Comment 5.6: *The players agree that they have played six points in the game but disagree over the score because they do not agree on who won the second point. The receiver acknowledges that the server called the score after each point and that the receiver did not express disagreement with the score until now. What should happen?* The score as announced by the server should prevail because the receiver did not object. Note, however, if the receiver denied hearing the score, then the official would have to be called to go through the normal 3-step process to settle the dispute.

USTA Comment 5.7: *When do players change ends?* Players change ends after every six points and at the Tiebreak. **See Rule 10.** They must change sides during the Tiebreak without any break or delay.

6. SCORE IN A SET (OLD 27)

There are different methods of scoring in a set. The two main methods are the "Advantage Set" and the "Tie-break Set". Either method may be used provided that the one to be used is announced in advance of the event. If the "Tie-break Set" method is to be used, it must also be announced whether the final set will be played as a "Tie-break Set" or an "Advantage Set".

> **USTA Comment:** *USTA Regulation I.V.1.a requires a 7-Point Tiebreak (first to 7 by a margin of 2) be played in all sets except when a 10-Point Tiebreak (first to 10 by a margin of 2) is played in lieu of the deciding final set.*

    a. "Advantage Set"

      The first player/team to win six games wins that "Set", provided there is a margin of two games over the opponent(s). If necessary, the set shall continue until this margin is achieved.

    b. "Tie-break Set"

      The first player/team to win six games wins that "Set", provided there is a margin of two games over the opponent(s). If the score reaches six games all, a tie-break game shall be played.

Additional approved alternative scoring methods can be found in **Appendix IV**.

7. SCORE IN A MATCH (OLD 28)

A match can be played to the best of 3 sets (a player/team needs to win 2 sets to win the match) or to the best of 5 sets (a player/team needs to win 3 sets to win the match).

8. SERVER & RECEIVER (OLD 5)

The players/teams shall stand on opposite sides of the net. The server is the player who puts the ball into play for the first point. The receiver is the player who is ready to return the ball served by the server.

Case 1: Is the receiver allowed to stand outside the lines of the court?

Decision: Yes. The receiver may take any position inside or outside the lines on the receiver's side of the net.

9. CHOICE OF ENDS & SERVICE (OLD 6)

This choice of ends and the choice to be server or receiver in the first game shall be decided by toss before the warm-up starts. The player/team who wins the toss may choose:

    a. To be server or receiver in the first game of the match, in which case the opponent(s) shall choose the end of the court for the first game of the match; or

    b. The end of the court for the first game of the match, in which case the opponent(s) shall choose to be server or receiver for the first game of the match; or

    c. To require the opponent(s) to make one of the above choices

Case 1: Do both players/teams have the right to new choices if the warm-up is stopped and the players leave the court?

Decision: Yes. The results of the original toss stands, but new choices may be made by both players/teams.

> **USTA Comment 9.1:** *When should the toss be made?* The toss should be made before the warm-up so that the players can warm-up on the same side from which they play their first game.

10. CHANGE OF ENDS (OLD 16 & 27)

The players shall change ends at the end of the first, third, and every subsequent odd game of each set. The players shall also change ends at the end of each set unless the total number of games in that set is even, in which case the players change ends at the end of the first game of the next set.

During a tie-break game, players shall change ends after every six points.

> **USTA Comment 10.1:** *Do the players change sides after a tiebreak is played to decide a set?* Yes.

> **USTA Comment 10.2:** *When do the players change sides during a tiebreak that uses the Coman Tiebreak Procedure?* The Coman Tiebreak Procedure is identical to the regular procedure except that the players change ends after the first point, then after every four points, and at the conclusion of the Tiebreak.

11. BALL IN PLAY (OLD 17)

Unless a fault or a let is called, the ball is in play from the moment the server hits the ball, and remains in play until the point is decided.

> **USTA Comment 11.1:** *Is a point decided when a good shot has clearly passed a player, or when an apparently bad shot passes over the baseline or sideline?* No. A ball is in play until it bounces twice or lands outside the court, hits a permanent fixture, or hits a player. A ball that becomes imbedded in the net is out of play.

> **USTA Comment 11.2:** *Must an out call on a player's shot to the opponent's court be made before the opponent's return has either gone out of play or been hit by the first player?* Yes.

12. BALL TOUCHES A LINE (OLD 22)

If a ball touches a line, it is regarded as touching the court bounded by that line.

> **USTA Comment 12.1:** *If a player cannot call a ball out with certainty, should the player regard the ball as good?* Yes. **The Code § 6 & 8** require a player to give the opponents the benefit of any doubts.

13. BALL TOUCHES A PERMANENT FIXTURE (OLD 23)

If the ball in play touches a permanent fixture after it has hit the correct court, the player who hit the ball wins the point. If the ball in play touches a permanent fixture before it hits the ground, the player who hit the ball loses the point.

> **USTA Comment 13.1:** *What happens if a ball hits the top of the net outside the singles stick and then lands in the court?* The player who hit the ball loses the point because the ball hit a permanent fixture. In singles the area outside the singles stick is a permanent fixture.

> **USTA Comment 13.2:** *Who wins the point if a player hits a ball that hits an object attached to the net or post (such as the scoring device) and then lands in the proper court?* The player who hit the ball loses the point because it hit a permanent fixture before landing in the court.

14. ORDER OF SERVICE (OLD 15 & 35)

At the end of each standard game, the receiver shall become the server and the server shall become the receiver for the next game.

In doubles, the team due to serve in the first game of each set shall decide which player shall serve for that game. Similarly, before the second game starts, their opponents shall decide which player shall serve for that game. The partner of the player who served in the first game shall serve in the third game and the partner of the player who served in the second game shall serve in the fourth game. This rotation shall continue until the end of the set.

15. ORDER OF RECEIVING IN DOUBLES (OLD 35, 36, & 40)

The team which is due to receive the first game of a set shall decide which player shall receive the first point in the game. Similarly, before the second game starts, their opponents shall decide which player shall receive the first point of that game. The player who was the receiver's partner for he first point of the game shall receive the second point and this rotation shall continue until the end of he game and the set.

After the receiver has returned the ball, either player in a team can hit the ball.

Case 1: Is one member of a doubles team allowed to play alone against the opponents?

Decision: No.

16. THE SERVICE (OLD 7)

Immediately before starting the service motion, the server shall stand at rest with both feet behind (i.e. further from the net than) the baseline and within the imaginary extensions of the centre mark and the sideline.

The server shall then release the ball by hand in any direction and hit the ball with the racket before the ball hits the ground. The service motion is completed at the moment that the player's racket hits or misses the ball. A player who is able to use only one arm may use the racket for the release of the ball.

17. SERVING (OLD 9 & 27)

When serving in a standard game, the server shall stand behind alternate halves of the court, starting from the right half of the court in every game.

In a tie-break game, the service shall be served from behind alternate halves of the court, with the first service from the right half of the court.

The service shall pass over the net and hit the service court diagonally opposite, before the receiver returns it.

18. FOOT FAULT (OLD 7 & 8)

During the service motion, the server shall not:
  a. Change position by walking or running, although slight movements of the feet are permitted; or
  b. Touch the baseline or the court with either a foot; or
  c. Touch the area outside the imaginary extension of the sideline with either foot; or
  d. Touch the imaginary extension of the centre mark with either foot.
If the server breaks this rule it is a "Foot Fault".
Case 1: In a singles match, is the server allowed to serve standing behind the part of the baseline between the singles sideline and the doubles sideline?
Decision: No.
Case 2: Is the server allowed to have one or both feet off the ground?
Decision: Yes.

- A server who takes more than one step with either foot after the "feet at rest" position described above is at risk for being called for a foot fault. The serve becomes a foot fault when, in the judgement of an experienced official, the server has materially changed position before or during any racket or arm motion.
- A server whose footwork changes significantly from one serve to the next is at risk for being called for a foot fault.
- Serves that look like the running volleyball serve violate the rule. Serves in which the server runs or walks from a point well behind the baseline to the baseline are also illegal, as are serves in which the server walks or runs along the baseline before choosing a spot from which to deliver the serve.

USTA Comment 18.3: *When does a foot fault occur?* A player commits a foot fault if after the player's feet are at rest but before the player strikes the ball, either foot touches:
- the court, including the baseline;
- any part of the imaginary extension of the center mark; or
- beyond the imaginary extension of the outside of the singles sideline in singles or the doubles sideline in doubles.

USTA Comment 18.4: *Is it a foot fault if the server's foot touches the baseline and then the server catches the tossed ball instead of attempting to strike it?* This is not a foot fault as long as the server makes no attempt to strike the ball.

USTA Comment 18.5: *May a player ask an official how he foot faulted?* Yes. The official should then give a brief answer.

USTA Comment 18.6: *When may the receiver or the receiver's partner call foot faults?* In a non-officiated match, the receiver or the receiver's partner may call foot faults after all efforts (warning the server and attempting to locate an official) have failed and the foot faulting is so flagrant as to be clearly perceptible from the receiver's side.

19. SERVICE FAULT (OLD 10 & 39)
The service is a fault if:
a. The server breaks rules **16, 17, or 18**; or
b. The server misses the ball when trying to hit it; or
c. The ball served touches a permanent fixture, singles stick or net post before it hits the ground; or
d. The ball served touches the server or the server's partner, or anything the server or server's partner is wearing or carrying.

Case 1: After tossing a ball to serve, the server decides not to hit it and catches it instead. Is this a fault?
Decision: No. A player who tosses the ball and then decides not to hit it, is allowed to catch the ball with the hand or the racket, or to let the ball bounce.
Case 2: During a singles match played on a court with net posts and singles sticks, the ball served hits a singles stick and then hits the correct service court. Is this a fault?
Decision: Yes.

20. SECOND SERVICE (OLD 11)

If the first service is a fault, the server shall serve again without delay from behind the same half of the court from which that fault was served, unless the service was from the wrong half.

> **USTA Comment 20.1:** *Before returning the second serve, may the receiver clear a ball from a first service fault that has rebounded onto the playing area?* Yes.

21. WHEN TO SERVE & RECEIVE (OLD 12 & 30)

The server shall not serve until the receiver is ready. However, the receiver shall play to the reasonable pace of the server and shall be ready to receive within a reasonable time of the server being ready.

A receiver who attempts to return the service shall be considered as being ready. If it is demonstrated that the receiver is not ready, the service cannot be called a fault.

> **USTA Comment 21.1:** *Does this rule apply to the first and second serve?* Yes. This rule applies separately to both the first and second serve.
>
> **USTA Comment 21.2:** *Once ready, can the receiver become unready?* The receiver cannot become unready unless outside interference occurs.
>
> **USTA Comment 21.3:** *May the server hit the serve just as the receiver looks up after getting into the ready position?* No. The receiver is not ready until the receiver is in the ready position and has a second or two to make eye contact with the server.
>
> **USTA Comment 21.4:** *How much time may elapse from the moment the ball goes out of play at the end of the point until the serve is struck to start the next point?* When practical this time should not exceed 20 seconds. This limit does not apply if a player has to chase a stray ball.
>
> **USTA Comment 21.5:** *Does the 20-second provision of Rule 29 apply to the second serve?* No. The server must strike the second serve without delay.
>
> **USTA Comment 21.6:** *Should the server be penalized for delay if the server was not tossing the ball until about 15 seconds after the end of the previous point even though the receive was ready within 10 seconds?* No. The server is entitled to establish the pace as long as it is reasonable. This means that the server has up to 20 seconds to put the ball in play.
>
> **USTA Comment 21.7:** *Should the receiver be penalized for delay if the receiver was not getting into ready position until 18 seconds after the end of the previous point even though the server was ready to serve within about 15 seconds?* Yes. The receiver is subject to a Time Violation. The receiver must play to the reasonable pace of the server. (A pace of 12 to 15 seconds is considered reasonable.)
>
> **USTA Comment 21.8:** *May the server suddenly increase the pace from 20 seconds to 12 seconds?* No. The server may speed up the pace only so long as the new pace is reasonable and only so long as the change does not occur suddenly.

22. THE LET DURING A SERVE (OLD 14)

The service is a let if:

a. The ball served touches the net, strap or band, and is otherwise good; or, after touching the net, strap or band, touches the receiver or the receiver's partner or anything they wear or carry before hitting the ground; or

b. The ball is served when the receiver is not ready.

In case of a service let, that particular service shall not count, and the server shall serve again, but a service let does not cancel a previous fault.

23. THE LET (OLD 13 & 25)

In all cases when a let is called, except when a service let is called on a second service, the whole point shall be replayed.

Case 1: When the ball is in play, another ball rolls onto court. A let is called. The server had previously served a fault. Is the server now entitled to a first service or second service?

Decision: First service. The whole point must be replayed.

24. PLAYER LOSES POINT (OLD 18, 19, 20 & 40)

The point is lost if:

a. The player serves two consecutive faults; or

b. The player does not return the ball in play before it bounces twice consecutively; or

c. The player returns the ball in play so that it hits the ground, or an object, outside the correct court; or

d. The player returns the ball in play so that, before it bounces, it hits a permanent fixture; or

e. The player deliberately carries or catches the ball in play on the racket or deliberately touches it with the racket more than once; or

f. The player or the racket, whether in the player's hand or not, or anything which the player is wearing or carrying touches the net, net posts/singles sticks, cord or metal cable, strap or band, or the opponent's court at any time while the ball is in play; or

g. The player hits the ball before it has passed the net; or

h. The ball in play touches the player or anything that the player is wearing or carrying, except the racket; or

i. The ball in play touches the racket when the player is not holding it; or

j. The player deliberately and materially changes the shape of the racket when the ball is in play; or

k. In doubles, both players touch the ball when returning it.

Case 1: After the server has served a first service, the racket falls out of the server's hand and touches the net before the ball has bounced. Is this a service fault, or does the server lose the point?

Decision: The server loses the point because the racket touches the net while the ball is in play.

Case 2: After the server has served a first service, the racket falls out of the server's hand and touches the net after the ball has bounced outside the correct service court. Is this a service fault, or does the server lose the point?

Decision: This is a service fault because when the racket touched the net the ball was no longer in play.

Case 3: In a doubles match, the receiver's partner touches the net before the ball that has been served touches the ground outside the correct service court. What is the correct decision?

Decision: The receiving team loses the point because the receiver's partner touched the net while the ball was in play.

Case 4: Does a player lose the point if an imaginary line in the extension of the net is crossed before or after hitting the ball?

Decision: The player does not lose the point in either case provided the player does not touch the opponent's court.

Case 5: Is a player allowed to jump over the net into the opponent's court while the ball is in play?

Decision: No. The player loses the point.

Case 6: A player throws the racket at the ball in play. Both the racket and the ball land in the court on the opponent's side of the net and the opponent(s) is unable to reach the ball. Which player wins the point?

Decision: The player who threw the racket at the ball loses the point.

Case 7: A ball that has just been served hits the receiver or in doubles the receiver's partner before it touches the ground. Which player wins the point?

Decision: The server wins the point, unless it is a service let.

Case 8: A player standing outside the court hits the ball or catches it before it bounces and claims the point because the ball was definitely going out of the correct court.

Decision: The player looses the point, unless it is a good return, in which case the point continues.

USTA Comment 24.1: *Does a player lose the point if the player's hat hits the net?* Yes. A player loses the point when any part of the player's body, equipment, or apparel touches the net.

USTA Comment 24.2: *What happens if the ball hits a player's hat that landed on the court earlier in the point?* The ball remains in play because the opponent did not ask for a let. When play continued after the hat landed on the court, the hat became part of the court. Therefore when a ball hits the hat, it is treated in the same manner as if the ball had hit the court.

USTA Comment 24.3: *If a player's hat falls off during a point, may the opponent stop play and claim a let?* Yes. The opponent's immediate request should be granted. A let should not be granted after the point nor should a request from the player who lost the hat.

USTA Comment 24.4: *What happens if a player's dampening device comes out and hits the net or the opponent's court?* The player loses the point unless the ball went out of play before the device hit the net or court. If the device is not discovered until after the point is over, the point stands as played.

USTA Comment 24.5: *Does a player lose a point if the ball hits his racket twice during one swing?* No. Only when there is a definite and deliberate "second push" by the player does the shot become illegal. "Deliberately" is the key word in this rule. Two hits occurring during a single continuous swing are not deemed a double hit.

USTA Comment 24.6: *Does the clashing of rackets make the return illegal?* No. Unless it is clear that more than one racket touched the ball.

USTA Comment 24.7: *Does a player who touches a pipe support that runs across the court at the bottom of the net lose the point?* Yes. The pipe support is considered a part of the net *except* when a ball hits it, in which case the pipe support is considered part of the court.

USTA Comment 24.8: *What happens if a player stretches to hit a ball, the racket falls to the ground, and the ball then goes into the court for a winner?* The player wins the point unless the racket was not in the player's hand at the instant the ball was struck.

25. A GOOD RETURN (OLD 24)

It is a good return if:

a. The ball touches the net, net posts/singles sticks, cord or metal cable, strap or band, provided that it passes over any of them and hits the ground within the correct court; except as provided in **Rule 2** and **24 (d)**; or

b. After the ball in play has hit the ground within the correct court and has spun or been blown back over the net, the player reaches over the net and plays the ball into the correct court, provided that the player does not break **Rule 24**; or

c. The ball is returned outside the net posts, either above or below the level of the top of the net, even though it touches the net posts, provided that it hits the ground in the correct court; except as provided in **Rules 2** and **24 (d)**; or

d. The ball passes under the net cord between the singles stick and the adjacent net post without touching either net, net cord or net post and hits the ground in the correct court; or

e. The player's racket passes over the net after hitting the ball on the player's own side of the net and the ball hits the ground in the correct court; or

f. The player hits the ball in play, which hits another ball lying in the correct court.

Case 1: A player returns a ball which then hits a singles stick and hits the ground in the correct court. Is this a good return?

Decision: Yes. However, if the ball is served and hits the singles stick, it is a service fault.

Case 2: A ball in play hits another ball which is lying in the correct court. What is the correct decision?

Decision: Play continues. However, if it is not clear that the actual ball in play has been returned, a let should be called.

USTA Comment 25.1: *What happens if the ball in play strikes a ball that came from another court after the start of the point?* Replay the point.

USTA Comment 25.2: *Must a request to remove a ball that is lying in the opponent's Court be honored?* Yes, but not while the ball is in play. Additionally, a request to remove a ball that is outside the Court reasonably close to the lines also must be honored.

USTA Comment 25.3: *In doubles is it a good return if a ball passes under the net cord and inside the post without touching either in a doubles match?* No. This is a "through."

USTA Comment 25.4: *Does a player lose the point if the opponent's ball touches a pipe support that runs across the court at the bottom of the net?* No. The pipe support is considered a part of the court *except that* it is considered part of the net when a player, or anything the player wears or carries, touches the pipe support.

26. HINDRANCE (OLD 21, 25 & 36)

If a player is hindered in playing the point by a deliberate act of the opponent(s), the player shall win the point.

However, the point shall be replayed if a player is hindered in playing the point by either an unintentional act of the opponent(s), or something outside the player's own control (not including a permanent fixture).

Case 1: Is an unintentional double hit a hindrance?

Decision: No. See also **Rule 24 (e)**.

Case 2: A player claims to have stopped play because the player thought that the opponent(s) was being hindered. Is this a hindrance?

Decision: No. The player loses the point.

Case 3: A ball in play hits a bird flying over the court. Is this a hindrance?

Decision: Yes, the point shall be replayed.

Case 4: During a point, a ball or other object that was lying on the player's side of the net when the point started hinders the player. Is this a hindrance?

Decision: No.

Case 5: In doubles, where are the server's partner and receiver's partner allowed to stand?

Decision: The server's partner and the receiver's partner may take any position on their own side of the net, inside or outside the court. However, if a player is creating a hinderance to the opponent(s), the hinderance rule should be used.

> **USTA Comment 26.1:** *What is the difference between a deliberate and an unintentional act?* Deliberate means a player did what the player intended to do, even if the result was unintended. An example is a player who advises the player's partner in such a loud voice that their opponents are hindered. Unintentional refers to an act over which a player has no control, such as a hat blowing off or a scream after a wasp sting.

> **USTA Comment 26.2:** *Can a player's own action be the basis for that player claiming a let or a hinderance?* No. Nothing a player does entitles that player to call a let. For example, a player is not entitled to a let because the player breaks a string, the player's hat falls off, or a ball in the player's pocket falls out.

> **USTA Comment 26.3:** *What happens if a player's cell phone rings while the ball is in play?* Because the player created the disturbance by bringing the phone to the court and not turning it off, the player is not entitled to a let. If the referee did not notify the players that cell phones should be turned off and if this is the first time that the phone has rung, then the opponent is entitled to a let. If the referee notified the players or if the player receives more than one call that rings, the opponent wins the point based on a hinderance.

> **USTA Comment 26.4:** *Can the server's discarding of a second ball constitute a hinderance?* Yes. If the receiver asks the server to stop discarding the ball, then the server shall stop. Any continued discarding of the ball constitutes a deliberate hinderance, and the server loses the point.

> **USTA Comment 26.5:** *Is an out call or other noise from a spectator a hinderance that allows a point to be replayed?* No. The actions of a spectator in an area designated for spectators is not the basis for replaying the point.

27. CORRECTING ERRORS (NEW)

As a principle, when an error in respect of the Rules of Tennis is discovered, all points previously played shall stand. Errors so discovered shall be corrected as follows:

a. (OLD 9a, 11, & 27b, iii)
During a standard game or a tie-break game, if a player serves from the wrong half of the court, this should be corrected as soon as the error is discovered and the server shall serve from the correct half of the court according to the score. A fault that was served before the error was discovered shall stand.

b. (OLD 16)
During a standard game or a tie-break game, if the players are at the wrong ends of the court, the error should be corrected as soon as it is discovered and the server shall serve from the correct end of the court according to the score.

c. (OLD 15 & 37)
If a player serves out of turn during a standard game, the player who was originally due to serve shall serve as soon as the error is discovered. However, if a game is completed before the error is discovered the order of service shall remain as altered.

A fault that was served by the opponent(s) before the error was discovered shall not stand.

In doubles, if the partners of one team serve out of turn, a fault that was served before the error was discovered shall stand.

d. (OLD 27, Case 3)

If a player serves out of turn during a tie-break game and the error is discovered after an even number of points have been played, the error is corrected immediately. If the error is discovered after an odd number of points have been played, the order of service shall remain as altered.

A fault that was served by the opponent(s) before the error was discovered shall not stand.

In doubles, if the partners of one team serve out of turn, a fault that was served before the error was discovered shall stand.

> **USTA Comment:** *Rule 27d. contains new language that clarified the old language. The results are unchanged.*

e. (OLD 38)

During a standard game or a tie-break game in doubles, if there is an error in the order of receiving, this shall remain as altered until the end of the game in which the error is discovered. For the next game in which they are the receivers in that set, the partners shall then resume the original order of receiving.

f. (OLD 27, Case 1)

If in error a tie-break game is started at 6 games all, when it was previously agreed that the set would be an "Advantage set", the error shall be corrected immediately if only one point has been played. If the error is discovered after the second point is in play, the set will continue as a "Tie-break set".

g. (OLD 27, Case 2)

If in error a standard game is started at 6 games all, when it was previously agreed that the set would be a "Tie-break set", the error shall be corrected immediately if only one point has been played. If the error is discovered after the second point is in play, the set will continue as an "Advantage set" until the score reaches 8 games all (or a higher even number), when a tie-break game shall be played.

h. (NEW)

If in error an "Advantage set" or "Tie-break set" is started, when it was previously agreed that the final set would be a deciding match tie-break, the error shall be corrected immediately if only one point has been played. If the error is discovered after the second point is in play, the set will continue either until a player or team wins three games (and therefore the set) or until the score reaches 2 games all, when a deciding match tie-break shall be played. However, if the error is discovered after the fifth game has started, the set will continue as a "Tie-break set". (See **Appendix IV**.)

i. (OLD 32)

If the balls are not changed in the correct sequence, the error shall be corrected when the player/team who should have served with new balls in next due to serve a new game. Thereafter the balls shall be changed so that the number of games between ball changes shall be that originally agreed. Balls should not be changed during a game.

USTA Comments on Correcting Errors

USTA Comment 27.1: Errors as to Ends, Sides, Rotation, and Service Order, Etc. The general guiding philosophy regarding any mistakes made by players in failing to change ends, serving from wrong ends, serving to the wrong court, receiving from the wrong court, etc., is this: Any such error shall be rectified as soon as discovered but not while the ball is in play, and any points completed under the erroneous condition shall be counted.

There are only three exceptions to the "rectify immediately" requirement. One is in the case of a doubles match where the players of one team happened to reverse their left court/right court receiving lineup in the middle of a set, and the switch is discovered in the middle of a game. In this case the players finish that game in the "new" positions, but resume their original lineup in all receiving games thereafter in that set.

The second is where a ball change has not taken place in proper sequence. **Rule 27i** now says that this mistake shall be corrected when the player , or pair in case of doubles, who should have served with the new balls is next due to serve. Do not change in mid-game.

The third occurs in a Tiebreak, either singles or doubles, in various situations.

USTA Comment 27.2: *The tournament announced on its entry form that the 10-point Tiebreak would be used in lieu of the third set. The players inadvertently play a regular Tiebreak Set until they realize the mistake at 3-0. What should happen?* Since the mistake was discovered before the start of the fifth game, pursuant to **Rule 27h** the player who is ahead 3-0 has won the set and the final set score should be shown as 3-0.

USTA Comment 27.3: *The tournament announced on its entry form that the 10-point Tiebreak would be used in lieu of the third set. The players inadvertently play a regular Tie-break Set until they realize the mistake at 2-1 and 30-all. What should happen?* Since the mistake was discovered before the start of the fifth game, the players must continue playing until the score reaches 3-1 or 2-2. If the score reaches 3-1, the player who is ahead wins the set and the final set score is recorded as 3-1. If the score reaches 2-2, a 10-point Tiebreak is played. The score is recorded as 3-2(x) with the score in the 10-point Tiebreak placed inside the parentheses.

USTA Comment 27.4: *The tournament announced on its entry form that the 10-point Tiebreak would be used in lieu of the third set. The players inadvertently play a regular Tiebreak Set until they realize the mistake after the server has served the first service fault to start the fifth game of the final set. What should happen?* Regardless of whether the score is 2-2, 3-1, or 4-0, the players must continue playing a full Tiebreak set because they have started the fifth game. If the score reaches 6-all the players would play a 7-point Tiebreak. The score is recorded the same as any other Tiebreak set.

USTA Comment 27.5: *Player A should have served the first point of the second set Tiebreak, but instead Player B served the first point. Pursuant to* **Rule 27d**, *the order of the service remained as altered. Who serves the first game of the final set?* Player B serves the first game. **Rule 5b** states that the players whose turn it was to serve first in the Set Tiebreak shall be the Receiver in the first game of the following set.

USTA Comment 27.6: *Same situation as in* **USTA Comment 27.5** *except that the 10-point Tiebreak is to be played in lieu of the third set. Who serves first in the 10-point Tiebreak that is to be played in lieu of the final set?* Player B.

USTA Comment 27.7: *The tournament announced that the 10-point 10-point Tiebreak would be played in lieu of the third set. The players split sets. With Player A ahead 7-5 in the 10-point Tiebreak, Player A comes to the net to shake hands with Player B. Player B refuses to shake hands because Player B contends that the 10-point Tiebreak is not over. What should happen?* The players should keep on playing because the 10-point Tiebreak is not yet over.

USTA Comment 27.8: *Same situation as in* **USTA Comment 27.7** *except that Player B shakes hands. The players report to the Referee that Player A won the Tiebreak 7-5. Does Player A win the match?* Yes. By shaking hands the players have acknowledged that they agreed the match was over. The 7-point Tiebreak was played in good faith so Player A wins the match, and the final set score should be recorded 1-0 (5).

28. ROLE OF COURT OFFICIALS (OLD 29)

For matches where officials are appointed, their roles and responsibilities can be found in **Appendix V.**

29. CONTINUOUS PLAY (OLD 29 & 30)

As a principle, play should be continuous, from the time the match starts (when the first service of the match is put in play) until the match finishes.

a. Between points, a maximum of twenty (20) seconds is allowed. When the players change ends at the end of a game, a maximum of ninety (90) seconds are allowed. However, after the first game of each set and during a tie-break game, play shall be continuous and the players shall change ends without a rest.

USTA Comment 29.1: *The 20-second time limit does not apply if a player has to chase a stray ball. See* **Rule 21** *and* **USTA Comments 21.1-9** *for more information about when the server and receiver must be ready.*

At the end of each set there shall be a set break of a maximum of one hundred and twenty (120) seconds.

The maximum time starts from the moment that one point finishes until the first service is struck for the next point.

Organizers of professional circuits may apply for ITF approval to extend the ninety (90) seconds allowed when the players change ends at the end of a game and the one hundred and twenty (120) seconds allowed at a set break.

b. If, for reasons outside the player's control, clothing, footwear or necessary equipment (excluding the racket) is broken or needs to be replaced, the player may be allowed reasonable extra time to rectify the problem.

c. No extra time shall be given to allow a player to recover condition. However, a player suffering from a treatable medical condition may be allowed one medical time-out of three minutes for the treatment of that medical condition. A limited number of toilet/change of attire breaks may also be allowed, if this is announced in advance of the event.

d. Event organizers may allow a rest period of a maximum of ten (10) minutes if this is announced in advance of the event. This rest period can be taken after the 3rd set in a best of 5 sets match, or after the 2nd set in a best of 3 sets match.

e. The warm-up time shall be a maximum of five (5) minutes, unless otherwise decided by the event organizers.

The match is resumed the next day. When Player A wins a long set, Player B claims entitlement to a rest period. Is Player B entitled to a rest period? No. Although this was the third set of the match, it was only the first set on that day. If there is a prolonged interruption, such as one caused by rain, and play is resumed on the same day, the players should be informed as to the point at which, if any, a rest period might be taken.

30. COACHING (OLD 31)

Coaching is considered to be communication, advice or instruction of any kind, audible or visible, to a player.

In team events where there is a team captain sitting on-court, the team captain may coach the player(s) during a set break and when the players change ends at the end of a game, but not when the players change ends after the first game of each set and not during a tie-break game.

In all other matches, coaching is not allowed.

Case 1: Is a player allowed to be coached, if the coaching is given by signals in a discreet way?

Decision: No.

Case 1: Is a player allowed to receive coaching when play is suspended?

Decision: Yes.

USTA Comment 30.1: A player may bring to the court written notes that were prepared before the start of the match and may read these notes during the match. Use of any device (e.g. cell phones, digital messaging systems, radios, mp3 players, cd and dvd players, cassette players, and watches that receive digital messages) to receive coaching and other information is prohibited.

USTA Comment 30.2: *Is coaching permitted during authorized rest periods?* Yes. However, an authorized rest period does not include a Toilet Break, a 20-minute Set Break, Medical Time-Out, Bleeding Time-Out, when play is suspended but the players remain on the court, when a player leaves the court seeking the assistance of the Referee, or when equipment or clothing is being adjusted.

USTA Comment 30.3: *Is coaching permitted in the USA League Programs?* No. Even though the USA League Programs are team competitions for adults and seniors, coaching is not permitted under league rules, except during authorized rest periods or as otherwise permitted.

RULES OF WHEELCHAIR TENNIS

The game of wheelchair tennis follows the ITF Rules of Tennis with the following exceptions.

a. The Two Bounce Rule

The wheelchair tennis player is allowed two bounces of the ball. The player must return the ball before it hits the ground a third time. The second bounce can be either in or out of the court boundaries.

b. The Wheelchair

The wheelchair is considered part of the body and all applicable rules, which apply to a player's body, shall apply to the wheelchair.

c. The Service

  i. The service shall be delivered in the following manner. Immediately before commencing the service, the server shall be in a stationary position. The server shall then be allowed one push before striking the ball.

  ii. The server shall throughout the delivery of the service not touch with any wheel, any area other than that behind the baseline within the imaginary extension of the centre mark and sideline.

  iii. If conventional methods for the service are physically impossible for a quadriplegic player, then the player or an individual may drop the ball for such a player. However, the same method of serving must be used each time.

d. Player Loses Point

A player loses a point if:

  i. The player fails to return the ball before it has touched the ground three times; or

  ii. Subject to rule e) below the player uses any part of his feet or lower extremities as breaks or as stabilizers while delivering service, stroking a ball, turning or stopping against the ground or against any wheel while the ball is in play; or

  iii. The player fails to keep one buttock in contact with his wheelchair seat when contacting the ball.

e. Propelling the Chair with the Foot

  i. If due to lack of capacity a player is unable to propel the wheelchair via the wheel then he may propel the wheelchair using one foot.

  ii. Even if in accordance with rule e) i. above a player is permitted to propel the chair using one foot, no part of the player's foot may be in contact with the ground:

  a) during the forward motion of the swing, including when the racket strikes the ball;

  b) from the initiation of the service motion until the racket strikes the ball.

  iii. A player in breach of this rule shall lose the point.

f. Wheelchair/Able-bodied Tennis

Where a wheelchair tennis player is playing with or against an able-bodied person in singles or doubles, the Rules of Wheelchair Tennis shall apply for the wheelchair player while the rules for Rules of Tennis for able-bodied tennis shall apply to the able-bodied player. In this instance, the wheelchair player is allowed two bounces while the able-bodied player is allowed only one bounce.

Note: The definition of lower extremities is: -the lower limb, including the buttocks, hip, thigh, leg, ankle and foot.

AMENDMENT TO THE RULES OF TENNIS

The official and decisive text to the Rules of Tennis shall be for ever in the English language and no alteration or interpretation of such Rules shall be made except at an Annual General Meeting of the Council, nor unless notice of the resolution embodying such alteration shall have been received by the Federation in accordance with Article 17 of the Constitution of the ITF Ltd (Notice of Resolutions) and such resolution or one having the like effect shall be carried by a majority of two-thirds of the votes recorded in respect of the same.

Any alteration so made shall take effect as from the first day of January following unless the Meeting shall be the like majority decide otherwise.

The Board of Directors shall have power, however, to settle all urgent questions of interpretation subject to confirmation at the General Meeting next following.

This Rule shall not be altered at any time without the unanimous consent of a General Meeting of the Council.

> **USTA Comment :** *The ITF, not the USTA is responsible for the Rules of Tennis. Amendments to the Rules of Tennis are made through the procedures of the ITF. Rule 69 of the ITF controls the manner in which amendments may be made to the Rules of Tennis. Amendments to the USTA Comments are made by the process described in* **USTA Regulation XII.H.**

APPENDIX I

THE BALL

a. The ball shall have a uniform outer surface consisting of a fabric cover and shall be white or yellow in colour. If there are any seams they shall be stitchless.

b. More than one type of ball is specified. The ball shall conform to the requirements shown in Table 1.

c. All test for rebound, size and deformation shall be made in accordance with the regulations below.

Case 1: Which ball type should be used on which court surface?

Decision: 3 different types of balls are approved for play under the Rules of Tennis, however:

a. Ball Type 1 (fast speed) is intended for play on slow pace court surfaces

b. Ball Type 2 (medium speed) is intended for play on medium/medium fast pace court surfaces.

c. Ball Type 3 (slow speed) is intended for play on fast pace court surfaces

TABLE 1. TENNIS BALL SPECIFICATIONS

	TYPE 1 (FAST)	TYPE 2 (MEDIUM)[1]	TYPE 3 (SLOW)[2]	HIGH ALTITUDE[3]
WEIGHT (MASS)	1.975-2.095 oz. (56.0-59.4 g.)	1.975-2.095 oz. (56.0-59.4 g.)	1.975-2.095 oz. (56.0-59.4 g.)	1.975-2.095 oz. (56.0-59.4 g.)
SIZE	2.575-2.700 in. (6.541-6.858 cm)	2.575-2.700 in. (6.541-6.858 cm)	2.575-2.875 in. (6.985-7.303 cm)	2.575-2.700 in. (6.541-6.858 cm)
REBOUND	53-58 in. (135-147 cm)	53-58 in. (135-147 cm)	53-58 in. (135-147 cm)	48-53 in. (22-135 cm)
FORWARD DEFORMATION[4]	0.195-0.235 in. (0.495-0.597 cm)	0.220-0.290 in. (0.559-0.737 cm)	0.220-0.290 in. (0.559-0.737 cm)	0.220-0.290 in. (0.559-0.737 cm)
RETURN DEFORMATION[4]	0.265-0.360 in. (0.673-0.914 cm)	0.315-0.425 in. (0.800-1.080 cm)	0.315-0.425 in. (0.800-1.080 cm)	0.315-0.425 in. (0.800-1.080 cm)

Notes:

[1] This ball may be pressurized or pressureless. The pressureless ball shall have an internal pressure that is no greater than 1 psi (7 kPa) and may be used for high altitude play above 4,000 feet (1,219m) above sea level and shall have been acclimatized for 60 days or more at the altitude of the specific tournament.

[2] This ball is also recommended for high altitude play on any court surface type above 4,000 feet (1,219m) above sea level.

[3] This ball is pressurized and is an additional ball specified for high altitude play above 4,000 feet (1,219m) above sea level only.

[4] The deformation shall be the average of a single reading along each of three perpendicular axes. No two individual readings shall differ by more than .030 inches (.076 cm).

REGULATIONS FOR MAKING TESTS

i. Unless otherwise specified all tests shall be made at a temperature of approximately 68° Fahrenheit (20° Celsius), a relative humidity of approximately 60% and, unless otherwise specified, an atmospheric pressure of approximately 30 inches Hg (102 kPa). All balls shall be removed from their container and kept at the recognized temperature and humidity for 24 hours prior to testing, and shall be at that temperature and humidity when the test is commenced.

ii. Other standards may be fixed for localities where the average temperature, humidity or average barometric pressure at which the game is being is being played differ materially from 68° Fahrenheit (20° Celsius), 60% relative humidity and 30 inches Hg (102 kPa) respectively.

Applications for such adjusted standards may be made by any National Association to the International Tennis Federation and, if approved, shall be adopted for such localities.

iii. In all tests for diameter, a ring gauge shall be used consisting of a metal plate, preferably non-corrosive, of a uniform thickness of one-eighth of an inch (0.318 cm). In the case of Ball Type 1 (fast speed) and Ball Type 2 (medium speed) balls there shall be two circular openings in the plate measuring 2.575 inches (6.541 cm) and 2.700 inches (6.858 cm) in diameter respectively. In the case of Ball Type 3 (slow speed) balls there shall be two circular openings in the plate measuring 2.750 inches (6.985 cm) and 2.875 inches (7.303 cm) in diameter respectively. The inner surface of the gauge shall have a convex profile with a radius of one-sixteenth of an inch (0.159 cm). The ball shall not drop through the smaller opening by its own weight in any orientation and shall drop through the larger opening by its own weight in all orientations.

iv. In all tests for deformation conducted under Rule 3, the machine designed by Percy Herbert Stevens and patented in Great Britain under Patent No. 230250, together with the subsequent additions and improvements thereto, including the modifications required to take return deformations, shall be employed. Other machines may be specified which give equivalent readings to the Stevens machine and these may be used for testing ball deformation where such machines have been given approval by the International Tennis Federation.

v. The procedure for carrying out test is as follows and should take place in the order specified:

a. Pre-compression—before any ball is tested it shall be steadily compressed by approximately one inch (2.54 cm) on each of three diameters at right angles to one another in succession; this process is to be carried out three times (nine compressions in all). All test are to be completed within two hours of pre-compression.

b. Weight (mass) test.
c. Size test (as in paragraph iii, above).
d. Deformation test—the ball is placed in position on the modified Stevens machine so that neither platen of the machine is in contact with the cover seam. The contact weight is applied, the pointer and the mark brought level, and the dials set to zero. The test weight is placed on the beam in a position that is equivalent to a load of 18 lb (8.2 kg) on the ball, after which the wheel is turned at a uniform speed such that five seconds elapse from the instant the beam leaves its seat until the pointer is brought level with the mark. When turning ceases the reading is recorded (forward deformation). The wheel is turned again until figure ten is reached on the scale (one inch (2.54 cm) deformation). The wheel is then rotated in the opposite direction at a uniform speed (thus releasing pressure) until the beam pointer again coincides with the mark. After waiting ten seconds, the pointer is adjusted to the mark if necessary. The reading is then recorded (return deformation). This procedure is repeated on each ball across the two diameters at right angles to the initial position and to each other.
e. Rebound test (as above)—the ball is dropped from 100 inches (254 cm) onto a smooth rigid and horizontal surface. Measurements of both drop height and rebound height are to be taken from the surface to the bottom of the ball.

CLASSIFICATION OF COURT SURFACE PACE

The ITF test method used for determining the pace of a court surface is test method ITF CS 01/01 (ITF Surface Pace Rating) as described in the ITF publication entitled "An initial ITF study on performance standards for tennis court surfaces".

Court surfaces which are found to have an ITF surface Pace Rating of between 0 and 35 shall be classified as being Category 1 (slow pace). Examples of court surface types which conform to this classification will include most clay courts and other types of unbound mineral surface.

Court surfaces which are found to have an ITF Surface Pace Rating of between 30 and 45 shall be classified as being Category 2 (medium/medium-fast pace). Examples of court surface types which conform to this classification will include most hardcourts with various acrylic type coatings plus some textile surfaces.

Court surfaces which are found to have an ITF Surface Pace Rating of over 40 shall be classified as being Category 3 (fast pace). Examples of court surface types which conform to this classification will include most natural grass, artificial turf and some textile surfaces.

Note: The proposed overlap in ITF Surface Pace Rating values for the above categories is to allow some latitude in ball selection.

APPENDIX II
THE RACKET

a. The hitting surface, defined as the main area of the stringing pattern bordered by the points of entry of the strings into the frame or points of contact of the strings with the frame, whichever is the smaller, shall be flat and consist of a pattern of crossed strings connected to a frame and alternately interlaced or bonded where they cross. The stringing pattern must be generally uniform and, in particular, not less dense in the centre than in any other area. The racket shall be designed and strung such that the playing characteristics are identical on both faces. The racket shall be free of attached objects, protrusions and devices other than those utilized solely and specifically to limit or prevent wear and tear or vibration or, for the frame only, to distribute weight. These objects, protrusions and devices must be reasonable in size and placement for such purposes.

b. The frame of the racket shall not exceed 29.0 inches (73.7 cm) in overall length, including the handle. The frame of the racket shall not exceed 12.5 inches (3.17 cm) in overall width. The hitting surface shall not exceed 15.5 inches (39.4 cm) in overall length, and 11.5 inches (29.2 cm) in overall width.

c. The frame, including the handle, and the strings, shall be free of any device which makes it possible to change materially the shape of the racket, or to change the weight distribution in the direction of the longitudinal axis of the racket which would alter the swing moment of inertia, or to change deliberately any physical property which may affect the performance of the racket during the playing of a point. No energy source that in any way changes or affects the playing characteristics of a racket may be built into or attached to a racket.

APPENDIX III
ADVERTISING

1. Advertising is permitted on the net as long as it is placed on the part of the net that is within 3 feet (0.914 m) from the centre of the net posts and is produced in such a way that it does not interfere with the vision of the players or the playing conditions.

2. Advertising and other marks or material placed on the back and sides of the court shall be permitted unless it interferes with the vision of the players or the playing conditions.

3. Advertising and other marks or material placed on the court surface outside the lines is permitted unless it interferes with the vision of the players or the playing conditions.

4. Notwithstanding paragraphs (1), (2), and (3) above, any advertising marks or materials placed on the net or placed at the back and sides of the court, or on the court surface outside the lines may not contain white or yellow or other light colors that may interfere with the vision of the players or the playing conditions.

5. Advertising and other marks or material are not permitted on the court surface inside the lines of the court.

APPENDIX IV
ALTERNATIVE SCORING METHODS

SCORE IN A GAME:
"No-Ad" SCORING METHOD
This alternate scoring method may be used.

A No-Ad game is scored as follows with the server's score being called first:

No point	-	"Love"
First point	-	"15"
Second point	-	"30"
Third point	-	"40"
Fourth point	-	"Game"

If both players/teams have won three points each, the score is "Deuce" and a deciding point shall be played. The receiver(s) shall choose whether to receive the service from the right half or the left half of the court. In doubles, the players of the receiving team cannot change positions to receive this deciding point. The player/team who wins the deciding point wins the "Game".

In mixed doubles, the play of the same gender as the server shall receive the deciding point. The players of the receiving team cannot change positions to receive the deciding point.

> **USTA Comment IV.1:** *USTA Regulation I.V.11. authorizes the Referee to switch to No-Ad scoring before the start of any round without prior notice in all tournaments other than national junior championships after inclement weather or other factors cause the tournament to fall behind its published schedule.*

SCORE IN A SET:
1. "SHORT SETS"
The first player/team who wins four games wins that set, provided there is a margin of two games over the opponent(s). If the score reaches four games all, a tie-break game shall be played.

2. DECIDING MATCH TIE-BREAK (7 POINTS)
When the score in a match is one set all, or two sets all in best of five sets matches, one tie-break game shall be played to decide the match. This tie-break game replaces the deciding final set.

3. DECIDING MATCH TIE-BREAK (10 POINTS)
When the score in a match is one set all, or two sets all in best of five matches, one tie-break game shall be played to decide the match. This tie-break game replaces the deciding final set.

The player/team who first wins ten points shall win this match tie-break and the match provided there is a margin of two points over the opponent(s).

Note: *When using the deciding match tie-break to replace the final set:*
- *the original order of service continues.* ***(Rules 5 and 14)***
- *in doubles, the order of serving and receiving within the team may be altered, as in the beginning of each set.* ***(Rules 5 and 14)***
- *before the start of the deciding match tie-break there shall be a 120 seconds set break.*
- *balls should not be changed before the start of the deciding match tie-break even if a ball change is due.*

APPENDIX V
ROLE OF COURT OFFICIALS

The referee is the final authority on all questions of tennis law and the referee's decision is final.

In matches where a chair umpire is assigned, the chair umpire is the final authority on all questions of fact during the match.

The players have the right to call the referee to court if they disagree with a chair umpire's interpretation of tennis law.

In matches where a line umpires and net umpires are assigned, they make all calls (including foot-fault calls) relating to that line or net. The chair umpire has the right to overrule a line umpire or a net umpire if the chair umpire is sure that a clear mistake has been made. The chair umpire is responsible for calling any line (including foot-faults) or net where no line umpire or net umpire is assigned.

A line umpire who cannot make a call shall signal this immediately to the chair umpire who shall make a decision. If the line umpire can not make a call, or if there is no line umpire, and the chair umpire can not make a decision on a question of fact, the point shall be replayed.

In team events where the referee is sitting on-court, the referee is also the final authority on questions of fact.

Play may be stopped or suspended at any time the chair umpire decides it is necessary or appropriate.

The referee may also stop or suspend play in the case of darkness, weather or adverse court conditions. When play is suspended for darkness, this should be done at the end of a set, or after an even number of games have been played in the set in progress. After a suspension in play, the score and position of players on-court in the match shall stand when the match resumes.

The chair umpire or referee shall make the decision regarding continuous play and coaching in respect of any Code of Conduct that is approved and in operation.

Case 1: The chair umpire awards the server a first service after an overrule, but the receiver argues that it should be a second service, since the server had already served a fault. Should the referee be called to court to give a decision?

Decision: Yes. The chair umpire makes the first decision about questions of tennis law (issues relating to the application of specific facts). However, if a player appeals the chair umpire's decision, then the referee shall be called to make the final decision.

Case 2: A ball is called out, but the player claims that the ball was good. May the referee be called to court to make a decision?

Decision: No. The chair umpire makes the final decision on questions of fact (issues relating to what actually happened during a specific incident).

Case 3: Is a chair umpire allowed to overrule a line umpire at the end of a point if, in the chair umpire's opinion, a clear mistake was made earlier in the point?

Decision: No. A chair umpire may only overrule a line umpire immediately after the clear mistake has been made.

Case 4: A line umpire calls a ball "Out" and then the player argues that the ball was good. Is the chair umpire allowed to overrule the line umpire?

Decision: No. A chair umpire must never overrule as the result of the protest or appeal by a player.

Case 5: A line umpire calls a ball "Out". The chair umpire was unable to see clearly, but thought the ball was in. May the chair umpire overrule the line umpire?

Decision: No. The chair umpire may only overrule when sure that the line umpire made a clear mistake.

Case 6: Is a line umpire allowed to change the call after the chair umpire has announced the score?

Decision: Yes. If a line umpire realizes a mistake, a correction should be made as soon as possible provided it is not as the result of a protest or appeal of a player.

Case 7: If a chair umpire or line umpire calls "out" and then corrects the call to good, what is the correct decision?

Decision: The chair umpire must decide if the original "out " call was a hindrance to either player. If it was a hindrance, the point shall be replayed. If it was not a hindrance, the player who hit the ball wins the point.

Case 8: A ball is blown back over the net and the player correctly reaches over the net to try to play the ball. The opponent(s) hinders the player from doing this. What is the correct decision?

Decision: The chair umpire must decide if the hindrance was deliberate or unintentional and either awards the point to the hindered player or order the point to be replayed.

USTA Comment V.1: *What is the difference between a "question of fact" and a "question of law"?* "Questions of fact" involve whether a specific event happened. Examples include whether a ball is in, whether a ball touched a player, whether a ball bounced twice, and whether a Server's foot touched a baseline before the serve was struck. "Questions of law" involve the application of the rules or regulations to facts that have already been determined. Examples include determining whether an act was a hindrance; whether a player should have been assessed a code violation for misconduct; and the procedure for correcting errors in serving order, serving and receiving position, and ends.

BALL MARK INSPECTION PROCEDURES

1. Ball mark inspections can only be made on clay courts.
2. A ball mark inspection request by a player (team) shall be allowed only if the chair umpire cannot determine the call with certainty from his/her chair on either a point-ending shot or when a player (team) stops playing the point during a rally (returns are permitted but then the player must immediately stop).
3. When the chair umpire has decided to make a ball mark inspection, he/she should go down from the chair and make the inspection himself. If he/she does not know where the mark is, he/she can ask the line umpire for help in locating the mark, but then the chair umpire shall inspect it.

4. The original call or overrule will always stand if the line umpire and chair umpire cannot determine the location of the mark or if the mark is unreadable.
5. Once the chair umpire has identified and ruled on a ball mark, this decision is final and not appealable.
6. In clay court tennis the chair umpire should not be too quick to announce the score unless absolutely certain of the call. If in doubt, wait before calling the score to determine whether a ball mark inspection is necessary.
7. In doubles the appealing player must make his/her appeal in such a way that either play stops or the chair umpire stops play. If an appeal is made to the chair umpire then he/she must first determine that the correct appeal procedure was followed. If it was not correct or if it was late, then the chair umpire may determine that the opposing team was deliberately hindered.
8. If a player erases the ball mark before the chair umpire has made a final decision, he/she concedes the call.
9. A player may not cross the net to check a ball mark without being subject to the Unsportsmanlike provision of the Code of Conduct.

USTA Comment: See **FACom II.C-6** for additional procedures.

ELECTRONIC REVIEW PROCEDURES

At tournaments where an Electronic Review System is used, the following procedures should be followed for matches on courts where it is used.
1. A request for an Electronic Review of a line call or overrule by a player (team) shall be allowed only on either a point-ending shot or when a player (team) stops playing the point during a rally (returns are permitted but then the player must immediately stop).
2. The chair umpire should decide to use the Electronic Review when there is doubt about the accuracy of the line call or overrule. However, the chair umpire may refuse the Electronic Review if he/she believes that the player is making an unreasonable request or that it was not made in a timely manner.
3. In doubles the appealing player must make his/her appeal in such a way that either play stops or the chair umpire stops play. If an appeal is made to the chair umpire then he/she must first determine that the correct appeal procedure was followed. If it was not correct or if it was late, then the chair umpire may determine that the opposing team was deliberately hindered, in which case the appealing team loses the point.
4. The original call or overrule will always stand if the Electronic Review is unable, for whatever reason, to make a decision on that line call or overrule.
5. The chair umpire's final decision will be the outcome of the Electronic Review and is not appealable. If a manual choice is required for the system to review a particular ball impact, an official approved by the referee shall decide which ball impact is reviewed.

PLAN OF THE COURT

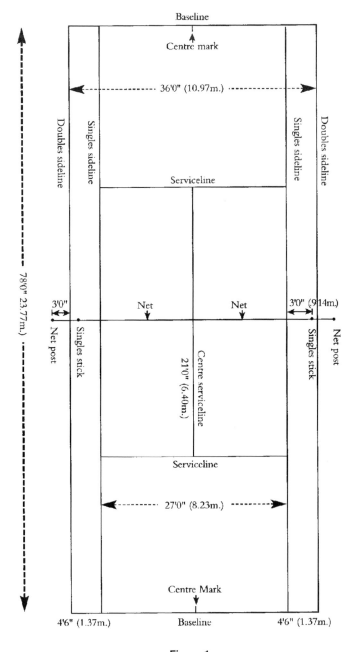

Figure 1

SUGGESTIONS ON HOW TO MARK OUT A COURT

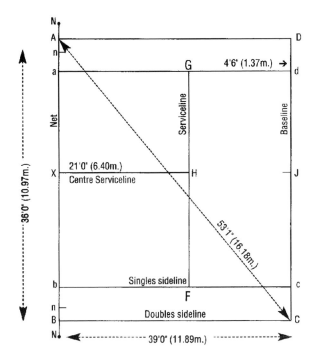

Figure 2

The following procedure is for the usual combined doubles and singles court. (See note at foot for a court for one purpose only.)

First select the position of the net; a straight line 42 feet (12.8 m) long. Mark the centre (X on the diagram above) and, measuring from there in each direction, mark:

at 13' 6" (4.11 m) the points a, b, where the net crosses the inner sidelines,
at 16' 6" (5.03 m) the positions of the singles sticks (n, n)
at 18' 0" (5.48 m) the points A, B, where the net crosses the outer sidelines,
at 21' 0" (6.40 m) the positions of the net posts (N, N), being the ends of the original 42' 0" (12.8 m) line

Insert pegs at A and B and attach to them the respective ends of two measuring tapes. On one, which will measure the diagonal of the half-court, take a length 53' 1" (16.18 m) and on the other (to measure the sideline) a length of 39' 0" (11.89 m). Pull both taut so that at these distances they meet at a point C, which is one corner of the court. Reverse the measurements to find the other corner D. As a check on this operation it is advisable at this stage to verify the length of the line CD which, being the baseline, should be found to be 36' 0" (10.97 m); and at the same time its centre J can be marked, and also the ends of the inner sidelines (c,d), 4' 6" (1.37 m) from C and D.

The centreline and serviceline are now marked by means of the points F, H, G, which are measured 21' 0" (6.40 m) from the net down the lines bc, XJ, ad, respectively.

Identical procedure the other side of the net completes the court.

If a singles court only is required, no lines are necessary outside the points a, b, c, d, but the court can be measured out as above. Alternatively, the corners of the baseline (c, d) can be found if preferred by pegging the two tapes at a and b instead of at A and B, and by then using lengths of 47' 5" (14.46 m) and 39' 0" (11.89 m). The net posts will be at n, n, and a 33' 0" (10 m) singles net should be used.

When a combined doubles and singles court with a doubles net is used for singles, the net must be supported at the points n, n, to a height of 3 feet 6 inches (1.07 m) by means of two singles sticks, which shall be not more than 3 inches (7.5 cm) square or 3 inches (7.5 cm) in diameter. The centres of the singles sticks shall be 3 feet (.914 m) outside the singles court on each side.

To assist in the placing of these singles sticks it is desirable that the points n, n, should each be shown with a white dot when the court is marked.

Note: As a guide for international competitions, the recommended minimum distance between the baselines and the backstops should be 21 feet (6.40 m) and between the sidelines and the sidestops the recommended minimum distance should be 12 feet (3.66 m).

As a guide for recreational and Club play, the recommended minimum distance between the baselines and backstops should be 18 feet (5.48 m) and between the sidelines and the sidestops the recommended minimum distance should be 10 feet (3.05 m).

As a guide, the recommended minimum height to the ceiling should be 30 feet (9.14 m).

USTA Comment L.1: Tennis Court Layout

All courts should be laid out for singles and doubles play. The same lines—except for the sideline extensions for doubles play—are required for each.

Courts in the northern two-thirds of the United States should generally be laid out with the long axis north and south; it is advantageous, however, to orient the courts in the southern one-third of the country 15°-25° west of true (not magnetic) north in order to minimize the adverse effects of the afternoon winter sun.

Figure 1 indicates the exact dimensions of the lines as well as recommended side and back spacing. Note that the dimensions shown in the diagram are measurements to the outside edge of the lines. For regulation play, the space behind the baseline (between the baseline and the fence) should not be less than 21 feet, for an overall dimension of 60' X 120'. For stadium courts, this perimeter spacing should be increased to allow space for the line umpires without impeding the players. Net posts should be located with their centers three feet outside the doubles sideline.

Most courts are laid out with lines two inches (2") wide. Lines may be one inch (1") to two inches (2") wide excepting the center service line which must be two inches (2") wide and the baselines which may be up to four inches (4") wide.

For more detailed information on the subject, *Tennis Courts,* a book containing United States Tennis Association and U. S. Tennis Court and Track Builders Association recommendations for the construction, maintenance, and equipment needs of a tennis court installation, can be obtained by contacting the USTA Bookstore, AT 888-832-8291.

THE CODE

THE PLAYER'S GUIDE FOR UNOFFICIATED MATCHES

PREFACE

When your serve hits your partner stationed at the net, is it a let, fault, or loss of point? Likewise, what is the ruling when your serve, before touching the ground, hits an opponent who is standing *back* to the baseline. The answers to these questions are obvious to anyone who knows the fundamentals of tennis, but it is surprising the number of players who don't know these fundamentals. All players have the responsibility to be familiar with the basic rules and customs of tennis. Further, it can be distressing when a player makes a decision in accordance with a rule and the opponent protests with the remark: "Well, I never heard of that rule before!" Ignorance of the rules constitutes a delinquency on the part of the player and often spoils an otherwise good match.

What is written here constitutes the essentials of *The Code,* a summary of procedures and unwritten rules that custom and tradition dictate all players should follow. No system of rules will cover every specific problem or situation that may arise. If players of good will follow the principles of *The Code,* they should always be able to reach an agreement, while at the same time making tennis more fun and a better game for all. The principles set forth in *The Code* shall apply in cases not specifically covered by the ITF Rules of Tennis and USTA Regulations.

Before reading this you might well ask yourself: Since we have a book that contains the rules of tennis, why do we need a code? Isn't it sufficient to know and understand all the rules? There are a number of things not specifically set forth in the rules that are covered by custom and tradition only. For example, if you have a doubt on a line call, your opponent gets the benefit of the doubt. Can you find that in the rules? Further, custom dictates the standard procedures that players will use in reaching decisions. These are the reasons we need a code.

—Col. Nick Powel

Note: *The Code* is not part of the official ITF Rules of Tennis. It is meant to be used as a guide for unofficiated matches. This edition of *The Code* is an adaptation of the original, which was written by Colonel Nicolas E. Powel.

PRINCIPLES

1. *Courtesy.* Tennis is a game that requires cooperation and courtesy from all participants. Make tennis a fun game by praising your opponents' good shots and by not:
   - conducting loud postmortems after points;
   - complaining about shots like lobs and drop shots;
   - embarrassing a weak opponent by being overly gracious or condescending:
   - losing your temper, using vile language, throwing your racet, or slamming a ball in anger; or
   - sulking when you are loosing.

2. *Counting points played in good faith.* All points played in good faith stand. For example, if after losing a point, a player discovers that the net was four inches too high, the point stands. If a point is played form the wrong court, there is no replay. If during a point, a player realizes that a mistake was made at the beginning (for example, service from the wrong court), the player shall continue playing the point. Corrective action may be taken only after a point has been completed.

THE WARM-UP

3. *Warm-up is not practice.* A player should provide the opponent a 5-minute warm-up (ten minutes if there are no ballpersons). If a player refuses to warm-up the opponent, the player forfeits the right to warm-up. Some players confuse warm-up and practice. Each player should make a special effort to hit shots directly to the opponent. (If partners want to warm each other up while their opponents are warming up, they may do so.)

4. *Warm-up serves and returns.* A player should take all warm-up serves before the first serve of the match. A player who returns serves should return them at a moderate pace in a manner that does not disrupt the server.

MAKING CALLS

5. *Player makes calls on own side of the net.* A player calls all shots landing on, or aimed at, the player's side of the net.

6. *Opponent gets benefit of doubt.* When a match is played without officials, the players are responsible for making decisions, particularly for line calls. There is a subtle difference between player decisions and those of an on-court official. An official impartially resolves a problem regarding a call, whereas a player is guided by the unwritten law that any doubt must be resolved in favor of the opponent. A player in attempting to be scrupulously honest on line calls frequently will find himself keeping a ball in play that might have been out or that the player discovers too late was out. *Even so, the game is much better played this way.*

7. *Ball touching any part of line is good.* If any part of the ball touches the line, the ball is good. A ball 99% out is still 100% good.

8. *Ball that cannot be called out is good.* Any ball that cannot be called out is considered to have been good. A player may not claim a let on the basis of not seeing a ball. One of tennis' most infuriating moments occurs after a long hard rally when a player makes a clean placement and the opponent says: "I'm not sure if it was good or out. Let's play a let." Remember, it is each player's responsibility to call all balls landing on, or aimed at, the player's side of the net. If a ball can't be called out with certainty, it is good. When you say your opponent's shot was really out but you offer to replay the point to give your opponent a break, you are deluding yourself because you must have had some doubt.

9. *Calls when looking across a line or when far away.* The call of a player looking down a line is much more likely to be accurate than that of a player looking across a line. When you are looking across a line, don't call a ball out unless you can clearly see part of the court between where the ball hit and the line. It is difficult for a player who stands on one baseline to question a call on a ball that landed near the other baseline.

10. *Treat all points the same regardless of their importance.* All points in a match should be treated the same. There is no justification for considering a match point differently than the first point.

11. *Requesting opponent's help.* When an opponent's opinion is requested and the opponent gives a positive opinion, it must be accepted. If neither player has an opinion, the ball is considered good. Aid from an opponent is available only on a call that ends a point.

12. *Out calls corrected.* If a player mistakenly calls a ball "out" and then realizes it was good, the point shall be replayed if the player returned the ball within the proper court. Nonetheless, if the player's return of the ball results in a "weak sitter," the player should give the opponent the point. If the player failed to make the return, the opponent wins the point. If the mistake was made on the second serve, the server is entitled to two serves.

13. *Player calls own shots out.* With the exception of the first serve, a player should call against himself or herself any ball the player clearly sees out regardless of whether requested to do so by the opponent. The prime objective in making calls is accuracy. All players should cooperate to attain this objective.

14. *Partners' disagreement on calls.* If doubles partners disagree about whether their opponents' ball was out, they shall call it good. It is more important to give your opponents the benefit of the doubt than to avoid possibly hurting your partner's feelings by not overruling. The tactful way to achieve the desired result is to tell your partner quietly of the mistake and then let your partner concede the point. If a call is changed from out to good, the point is replayed only if the ball that was called out was put back in play.

15. *Audible or visible calls.* No matter how obvious it is to a player that the opponent's ball is out, the opponent is entitled to a prompt audible or visible out call.

16. *Opponent's calls questioned.* When a player genuinely doubts an opponent's call, the player may ask: "Are you sure of your call?" If the opponent reaffirms that the ball was out, the call shall be accepted. If the opponent acknowledges uncertainty, the opponent loses the point. There shall be no further delay or discussion.

17. *Spectators never make calls.* A player shall not enlist the aid of a spectator in making a call. No spectator has part in the match.

18. *Prompt calls eliminate two chance option.* A player shall make all calls promptly after the ball has hit the court. A call shall be made either before the player's return shot has gone out of play or before the opponent has had the opportunity to play the return shot.

Prompt calls will quickly eliminate the "two chances to win the point" option that some players practice. To illustrate, a player is advancing to the net for an easy put away and sees a ball from the adjoining court rolling toward the court. The player continues to advance and hits the shot, only to have the supposed easy put away fly over the baseline. The player then claims a let. The claim is not valid because the player forfeited the right to call a let by choosing instead to play the ball. The player took a chance to win or lose and is not entitled to a second chance.

19. *Lets called when balls roll on the court.* When a ball from an adjacent court enters the playing area, the player shall call a let as soon as the player becomes aware of the ball. The player loses the right to call a let if the player unreasonably delays in making the call.

20. *Touches, hitting ball before it crosses net, invasion of opponent's court, double hits, and double bounces.* A player shall promptly acknowledge if:
- a ball touches the player;
- a player touches the net;
- the player touches the player's opponent's court;
- the player hits a ball before it crosses the net;
- the player deliberately carries or double hits the ball; or
- the ball bounces more than once in the player's court.

21. *Balls hit through the net or into the ground.* A player shall make the ruling on a ball that the player's opponent hits:
- through the net; or
- into the ground before it goes over the net.

22. *Calling balls on clay courts.* If any part of the ball mark touches the line on a clay court, the ball shall be called good. If you can see only part of the mark on the court, this means that the missing part is on the line or tape. A player should take a careful second look at any point-ending placement that is close to a line on a clay court. Occasionally a ball will strike the tape, jump, and then leave a full mark behind the line. This does not mean that a player is required to show the opponent the mark. The opponent shall not cross the net to inspect a mark. See **USTA Regulation I.N.8.** If the player hears the sound of the ball striking the tape and sees a clean spot on the tape near the mark, the player should give the point to the opponent.

SERVING

23. *Server's request for third ball.* When a server requests three balls, the receiver shall comply when the third ball is readily available. Distant balls shall be retrieved at the end of a game.

24. *Foot Faults.* A player may warn an opponent that the opponent has committed a flagrant foot fault. If the foot faulting continues, the player may attempt to locate an official. If no official is available, the player may call flagrant foot faults. Compliance with the foot fault rule is very much a function of a player's personal honor system. The plea that a Server should not be penalized because the server only just touched the line and did not rush the net is not acceptable. Habitual foot faulting, whether intentional or careless, is just as surely cheating as is making a deliberate bad line call.

25. *Service calls by serving team.* In doubles the receiver's partner should call the service line, and the receiver should call the sideline and the center service line. Nonetheless, either partner may call a ball that either clearly sees.

26. *Service calls by serving team.* Neither the server nor server's partner shall make a fault call on the first service even if they think it is out because the receiver may be giving the server the benefit of the doubt. There is one exception. If the receiver plays a first service that is a fault and does not put the return in play, the server or server's partner may make the fault call. The server and the server's partner shall call out any second serve that either clearly sees out.

27. *Service let calls.* Any player may call a service let. The call shall be made before the return of serve goes out of play or is hit by the server or the server's partner. If the serve is an apparent or near ace, any let shall be called promptly.

28. *Obvious faults.* A player shall not put into play or hit over the net an obvious fault. To do so constitutes rudeness and may even be a from of gamesmanship. On the other hand, if a player does not call a serve a fault and gives the opponent the benefit of a close call, the server is not entitled to replay the point.

29. *Receiver readiness.* The receiver shall play to the reasonable pace of the server. The receiver should make no effort to return a serve when the receiver is not ready. If a player attempts to return a serve (even if it is a "quick" serve), then the receiver (or Receiving team) is presumed to be ready.

30. *Delays during service.* When the server's second service motion is interrupted by a ball coming onto the court, the server is entitled to two serves. When there is a delay between the first and second serves:
- the server gets one serve if the server was the cause of the delay;
- the server gets two serves if the delay was caused by the Receiver or if there was outside interference.

The time it takes to clear a ball that comes onto the court between the first and second serves is not considered sufficient time to warrant the server receiving two serves unless this time is so prolonged as to constitute an interruption. The receiver is the judge of whether the delay is sufficiently prolonged to justify giving the server two serves.

SCORING

31. *Server announces score.* The server shall announce the game score before the first point of the game and the point score before each subsequent point of the game.

32. *Disputes.* Disputes over the score shall be resolved by using one of the following methods, which are listed in the order of preference:
- count all points and games agreed upon by the players and replay only the disputed points or games;
- play from a score mutually agreeable to all players;
- spin a racket or toss a coin.

HINDRANCE ISSUES

33. *Talking during a point.* A player shall not talk while the ball is moving toward the opponent's side of the court. If the player's talking interferes with an opponent's ability to play the ball, the player loses the point. Consider the situation where a player hits a weak lob and loudly yells at her partner to get back. If the shout is loud enough to distract the opponent, then the opponent may claim the point based on a deliberate hindrance.

34. *Feinting with the body.* A player may feint with the body while the ball is in play. A player may change position at any time, including while the server is tossing the ball. Any movement or sound that is made solely to distract an opponent, including, but not limited to, waving the arms or racket or stamping the feet, is not allowed.

35. *Lets due to hindrance.* A let is not automatically granted because of hindrance. A let is authorized only if the player could have made the shot had the player not been hindered. A let is also not authorized for a hindrance caused by something within a player's control. For example, a request for a let because the player tripped over the player's own hat should be denied.

36. *Grunting.* A player should avoid grunting and making other loud noises. Grunting and other loud noises may bother not only opponents but also players on adjacent courts. In an extreme case, an opponent or a player on an adjacent court may seek the assistance of the Referee or a Roving Umpire. The Referee or official may treat grunting and the making of loud noises as a hindrance. Depending upon the circumstances, this could result in a let or loss of point.

37. *Injury caused by a player.* When a player accidentally injures an opponent, the opponent suffers the consequences. Consider the situation where the server's racket accidentally strikes the receiver and incapacitates the receiver. The receiver is unable to resume play within the time limit. Even though the server caused the injury, the server wins the match by retirement.

On the other hand, when a player deliberately injures an opponent and affects the opponent's ability to play, then the opponent wins the match by default. Hitting a ball or throwing a racket in anger is considered a deliberate act.

WHEN TO CONTACT AN OFFICIAL

38. *Withdrawing from a match or tournament.* A player shall not enter a tournament and then withdraw when the player discovers that tough opponents have also entered. A player may withdraw from a match or tournament only because of injury, illness, or personal emergency. A player cannot play a match shall notify the Referee at once so that the opponent may be saved a trip. A player who withdraws from a tournament is not entitled to the return of the entry fee unless the player withdrew more than six days before the start of the tournament.

39. *Stalling.* The following actions constitute stalling:

- warming up longer than the allotted time;
- playing at about one-third a player's normal pace;
- taking more than 90 seconds on the odd-game changeover; or more than 120 seconds on the Set Break.
- taking longer than the authorized 10 minutes during a rest period;
- starting a discussion or argument in order for a player to catch his or her breath;
- clearing a missed first service that doesn't need to be cleared; and
- excessive bouncing of the ball before any serve.

A player who encounters a problem with stalling should contact an official. Stalling is subject to penalty under the Point Penalty System.

40. *Requesting an official.* While normally a player may not leave the playing area, the player may contact the Referee or a Roving Umpire to request assistance. Some reasons for visiting the Referee include:
- stalling;
- chronic flagrant foot faults;
- a Medical Time-Out
- a scoring dispute; and
- a pattern of bad calls.

A player may refuse to play until an official responds.

BALL ISSUES

41. *Retrieving stray balls.* Each player is responsible for removing stray balls and other objects from the player's end of the court. A player's request to remove a ball from the opponent's court must be honored. A player shall not go behind an adjacent court to retrieve a ball, nor ask a player for return of a ball from players on an adjacent court until their point is over. When a player returns a ball that comes from an adjacent court, the player shall wait until their point is over and then return it directly to one of the players, preferably the server.

42. *Catching a ball.* If a player catches a ball before it bounces, the player loses the point regardless of where the player is standing.

43. *New balls for a third set.* When a tournament specifies new balls for a third set, new balls shall be used unless all players agree otherwise.

MISCELLANEOUS

44. *Clothing and equipment malfunction.* If clothing or equipment, other than a racket, becomes unusable through circumstances outside the control of the player, play may be suspended for a reasonable period. The player may leave the court after the point is over to correct the problem. If a racket or string is broken, the player may leave the court to get a replacement, but the player is subject to code violations under the Point Penalty System.

45. *Placement of towels.* Place towels on the ground outside the net post or at the back fence. Clothing and towels should never be placed on the net.

If you have a rules problem, send full details, enclsoing a stamped self-addressed envelope, to USTA Tennis Rules Committe, c/o Officials Department, 70 West Red Oak Lane, White Plains, NY 10604-3602.

Reprinted by permission of the USTA

INDEX